India's Industrial Icons

India's Industrial Icons

Masters Of Manufacturing

Ehsan Sheroy

UNIEK ENTERPRISES

CONTENTS

INDEX

Introduction

In the huge embroidery of mankind's set of experiences, barely any countries have made as permanent an imprint on the world as India. With a rich social legacy going back centuries, this country has been a cauldron of development, imaginative articulation, and significant philosophical idea. However, India's effect on the worldwide stage isn't restricted to its old style customs alone. Throughout recent many years, it has quickly changed itself into an assembling force to be reckoned with, exhibiting wonderful ability in modern creation. This change has been driven by a blend of elements, including an immense pool of gifted work, a quickly developing homegrown market, and a guarantee to embracing current innovations.

In this investigation of India's modern symbols, we dig into the captivating universe of Indian assembling, looking at the powers that have molded the country's ascent in this circle and the people and organizations that have arisen as persuasive modern pioneers. This is a story of variation, development, and versatility — an account of visionary business people and determined industry skippers who have reclassified the nation's put on the worldwide monetary stage.

As we venture through the pages of this story, it is fundamental to consider the authentic scenery against which India's modern change has unfurled. The country's set of experiences is an embroidery woven with strings of old insight and progress, set apart by stupendous domains and celebrated traditions. However, the India of the 21st century is boundlessly unique in relation to the India of bygone eras. It remains as a cutting edge republic, embracing a majority rules system, secularism, and unregulated economy standards. This progress isn't just political yet has profound financial and modern underpinnings.

India's modern process can be partitioned into unmistakable stages. The post-freedom time, following India's independence from English pilgrim rule in 1947, denoted a time of financial independence and internal looking strategies. The nation looked to lay out homegrown businesses to meet its blossoming needs and diminish reliance on imported products. This period saw the foundation of a few public area endeavors (PSUs) in different enterprises, going from weighty assembling to framework improvement. While these drives made a base for modern turn of events, they likewise led to difficulties like organization, failure, and protectionism.

The 1991 financial changes, frequently alluded to as India's "monetary progression," proclaimed another period of financial change. These changes, driven by an extreme equilibrium of installments emergency, presented major developments in India's financial strategies, including diminished exchange hindrances, privatization, and unfamiliar venture progression. This change in strategy released a rush of business venture and development, permitting private players to assume a more significant part in India's modern scene. Thus, the Indian assembling area started to take on a more cutthroat and worldwide aspect.

A vital part of India's modern scene is its capacity to use its segment profit. India flaunts a huge, youthful, and trying labor force, making it a force to be reckoned with of work assets. This segment advantage has drawn in worldwide organizations, making India a center for offshoring, especially in data innovation (IT) and business process re-appropriating (BPO). The IT area, specifically, has been a noteworthy example of overcoming adversity, with Indian organizations and experts procuring a standing for their mastery and unwavering quality.

The outcome of the Indian IT industry not just shown India's true capacity as an assembling and specialist co-op yet additionally featured the significance of a gifted labor force and an empowering climate for organizations to flourish. Throughout the long term, this acknowledgment has driven a huge spotlight on training and expertise improvement, fully intent on supporting ability and encouraging development.

While the IT area has been a model of India's true capacity, it is in no way, shape or form the main example of overcoming adversity in Indian assembling. The country's ability stretches out to different ventures, from drugs and car assembling to materials and aviation. Indian organizations have left their imprint on homegrown soil as well as on the worldwide stage, contending with laid out global players. It is these heroes of industry that we will investigate in this account — India's modern symbols.

One Industry that has ascended to noticeable quality is India's drug area. Frequently alluded to as the "Drug store of the World," India has turned into a significant worldwide provider of nonexclusive medications. The area's development is credited to a mix of variables, including the accessibility of gifted researchers and designers, a powerful administrative system, and the capacity to create top notch drugs for a portion of the expense contrasted with Western nations. Indian drug organizations have not just met the medical care needs of the country yet have likewise sent out prescriptions to different regions of the planet, procuring a standing for moderateness and dependability.

In the realm of cars, India's rise as a significant assembling center is another surprising accomplishment. Home to a portion of the world's driving car producers, India has turned into a critical player in the worldwide auto industry. The Indian auto area isn't just known for creating financially savvy vehicles yet in addition for its plan and designing abilities. A few Indian vehicle makers have transformed the worldwide field, demonstrating that India can make items that are both excellent and seriously estimated.

The material business is one more area that has been fundamental to India's modern scene for a really long time. From the impeccable silks and cottons of antiquated India to the contemporary material assembling units, this industry has gone through critical change. Indian materials are eminent for their variety, craftsmanship, and rich customs.

In the cutting edge time, the area has adjusted to the requests of global business sectors while saving its social legacy. Indian material makers have kept a fragile harmony among custom and development, in this manner making progress on a worldwide scale.

Aviation and safeguard are one more domain in which India has taken huge steps. With a developing accentuation on native innovative work, India has seen the rise of effective aviation and guard organizations. These elements have made significant commitments to the country's guard capacities and have likewise wandered into the worldwide market, fabricating a scope of aviation items, from warrior airplane to satellite innovation.

As we dig further into India's modern process, it is difficult to overlook the pretended by visionary business people and industry pioneers. These people have fabricated effective ventures as well as roused another age of pioneers and business pioneers. Their accounts are stories of desire, assurance, and tenacious quest for greatness.

One such notorious figure is Jamsetji Goodbye, frequently alluded to as the "Father of Indian Industry." He established the Goodbye Gathering in the late nineteenth hundred years, which has since developed into one of India's biggest and most enhanced combinations. Goodbye's vision reached out past business to envelop cultural government assistance, apparent in the foundation of establishments like the Indian Organization of Science and Goodbye Foundation of Basic Exploration. The Goodbye Gathering's obligation to morals, manageability, and country building has set a benchmark for Indian organizations.

Likewise, Dhirubhai Ambani, the organizer behind Dependence Enterprises, is one more transcending figure in India's modern history. He rose from humble starting points to construct a rambling domain that traverses areas as different as petrochemicals, media communications, and retail. Ambani's story is a demonstration of the force of innovative soul and assurance, and his commitments to India's modern development stay huge.

In the drug area, the Reddy family, drove by Dr. Anji Reddy, assumed a significant part in laying out Dr. Reddy's Labs, a worldwide drug organization known for its exploration and assembling capacities. Dr. Reddy's vision of making prescriptions more reasonable and open has been instrumental in India's rise as a worldwide drug center point.

Anand Mahindra, the Director of the Mahindra Gathering, is another modern illuminating presence whose vision has been instrumental in the gathering's enhancement and worldwide extension. Mahindra's administration and spotlight on manageability and development have situated the gathering as a forerunner in areas like vehicles, aviation, and data innovation.

In the realm of data innovation, any semblance of N.R. Narayana Murthy, the prime supporter of Infosys, and Azim Premji, the Executive of Wipro, have been instrumental in laying out India as an IT force to be reckoned with.

These visionaries fabricated effective IT organizations as well as set an elevated expectation for corporate administration and moral strategic policies, procuring the trust of clients around the world.

India's modern process isn't without its difficulties and intricacies. In spite of noteworthy advancement, the nation faces various issues that request consideration. Foundation bottlenecks, administrative noise, and ability holes keep on presenting obstacles for the assembling area. Moreover, ecological manageability and mindful strategic policies have become basic worries in a world progressively aware of environmental change and social obligation. It is basic for India's modern symbols and arising pioneers to address these difficulties and add to the country's reasonable and comprehensive development.

Chapter 1

The Genesis of Indian Manufacturing Excellence

The historical backdrop of assembling in India is a story that traverses centuries, winding around together the strings of custom, development, and flexibility. From antiquated craftsmanship and exchange along the Silk Street to the ascent of present day ventures, India's assembling scene has gone through significant changes. This excursion includes both customary distinctive practices and contemporary innovative creation, mirroring a dynamic and various country.

India's assembling heritage can be followed back to the earliest known human civic establishments on the subcontinent. The Indus Valley Development, one of the world's most established metropolitan civic establishments, thrived around 2500 BCE. This old development showed wonderful abilities in metallurgy, earthenware, materials, and dot making, establishing the groundwork for India's standing as an assembling center point. The Indus Valley individuals participated in perplexing exchange organizations, sending out their products to Mesopotamia, Sumer, and other far off districts, making a diagram for India's getting through heritage as a focal point of creation and exchange.

The ensuing hundreds of years saw the advancement of assembling strategies, with every period making some meaningful difference. The Mauryan and Gupta realms, for example, made critical commitments to metallurgy and material creation. These early progressions set up for India's development as an assembling force to be reckoned with in the pre-current world.

During the middle age time frame, India's skill in assembling became known all over. The craft of material creation arrived at amazing levels, with fine textures like Muslin and Jamdani acquiring recognition. The Mughal Realm, which governed over a significant piece of the Indian subcontinent, assumed a critical part in cultivating fabricating greatness. Mughal sovereigns like Akbar the Incomparable were benefactors of expressions and artworks, advancing craftsmanship in different spaces, including materials, gems, and ceramics.

One of the most famous traditions of Mughal producing is the Taj Mahal, a work of art of design and creative magnificence. The development of this sepulcher embodies the complicated craftsmanship and scrupulousness that noticeable Mughal producing. Talented craftsmans and skilled workers were key to its creation, displaying the mix of design designing and imaginative artfulness.

The frontier period, set apart by the appearance of the English East India Organization in the seventeenth 100 years, achieved massive changes in India's assembling scene. While the English provincial rule significantly affected Indian culture, economy, and legislative issues, it likewise added to the change of assembling. The English presented automation and current assembling procedures, which would establish the groundwork for India's future modern turn of events.

Nonetheless, the English frontier rule was likewise portrayed by double-dealing, financial channel, and exchange arrangements that inclined toward the English to the detriment of India. The strategies of the English Raj were essentially designed for extricating India's assets to serve the pioneer aces. This double-dealing and the related deindustrialization prompted huge monetary difficulties for the Indian subcontinent.

The battle for autonomy from frontier rule, which finished in India's hard-battled opportunity in 1947, assumed a significant part in molding the country's modern scene. The longing for confidence and monetary strengthening prompted the foundation of another time of modern turn of events. The post-freedom years saw a change in the focal point of Indian assembling from agrarian and high quality to modern, with an accentuation on independence.

One of the principal significant achievements in post-autonomy Indian assembling was the foundation of public area endeavors (PSUs). These administration possessed organizations were laid out to advance the improvement of key ventures and lessen India's reliance on imports. The PSUs assumed an essential part in areas like large equipment, steel, and framework improvement.

The Indian government's Five-Year Plans, started in 1951, expected to direct the country's financial turn of events, including the development of assembling ventures. These plans set focuses for modern development, zeroing in on areas like energy, transportation, and large equipment. This period saw a critical accentuation on "blended economy" standards, joining components of communism and private enterprise to advance both state-possessed and confidential undertakings.

The Green Unrest, which started during the 1960s, denoted one more defining moment in Indian assembling. This rural change, powered by the presentation of high-yielding harvest assortments and current farming methods, expanded horticultural creation as well as provoked an interest for hardware and other fabricated products. The Green Transformation was a demonstration of India's capacity to adjust and enhance in light of evolving conditions.

The 1991 monetary changes, frequently alluded to as "progression" or "financial advancement," introduced another time of assembling in India. These changes were a reaction to an extreme equilibrium of installments emergency and a developing acknowledgment that the protectionist strategies of the past were hampering financial development. The changes included a huge decrease in exchange hindrances, privatization of state-possessed undertakings, and progression of unfamiliar speculation.

The progression strategies made India's ways for worldwide exchange, unfamiliar venture, and rivalry, bringing about a flood of private area cooperation in assembling. Indian organizations were not generally restricted to the homegrown market; they started to investigate global open doors, and unfamiliar organizations entered the Indian market. The change was especially obvious in businesses like data innovation (IT), media communications, and cars.

The IT and programming administrations area, specifically, arose as a force to be reckoned with of Indian assembling greatness. Indian IT organizations like Goodbye Consultancy Administrations (TCS), Infosys, and Wipro, rose to worldwide conspicuousness as suppliers of programming and IT administrations. These organizations utilized India's gifted labor force, capability in English, and cutthroat valuing to serve worldwide clients, changing India into a worldwide IT center.

The auto business was another area that went through a huge change. Indian auto makers, like Goodbye Engines, Mahindra and Mahindra, and Maruti Suzuki, extended their item portfolios, working on quality and plan to contend both locally and universally. The car area's outcome in assembling vehicles that joined quality and reasonableness made it a noteworthy illustration of Indian assembling ability.

The drug business, frequently alluded to as the "Drug store of the World," additionally took critical steps. Indian drug organizations became pioneers in the creation of conventional medications, giving reasonable medical services arrangements not exclusively to the Indian populace yet additionally to the global market. Organizations like Dr. Reddy's Labs and Cipla acquired worldwide acknowledgment for their commitments to medical services.

The development and enhancement of Indian assembling additionally stretched out to areas like materials, aviation, and protection. The material business, with its rich legacy, modernized and adjusted to satisfy the needs of worldwide business sectors.

Indian aviation and safeguard organizations wandered into the assembling of airplane, space innovation, and protection gear, adding to India's confidence in these basic areas.

The approach of the 21st century carried new moves and open doors to Indian assembling. The computerized upset and the ascent of Industry 4.0, portrayed by the incorporation of advanced advances into assembling processes, incited Indian organizations to adjust and enhance. Ideas like mechanization, man-made reasoning (computer based intelligence), and the Web of Things (IoT) started to reclassify the assembling scene.

As well as embracing innovation, Indian assembling began zeroing in on maintainability and natural obligation. As environmental change and natural worries acquired unmistakable quality, organizations started to take on greener practices and harmless to the ecosystem innovations. Manageable assembling cycles and items became key elements in keeping up with and growing piece of the pie.

The "Make in India" crusade, sent off in 2014, denoted one more critical achievement in India's excursion toward assembling greatness. This drive intended to change India into a worldwide assembling center by advancing homegrown creation, improving simplicity of carrying on with work, and drawing in unfamiliar speculation. "Make in India" looked to use India's segment profit and different ability pool to reinforce producing across areas, from hardware to guard gear.

In equal, India's obligation to advancement and innovative work (Research and development) has developed further. The public authority has started projects to empower development and business venture, supporting new companies and encouraging a culture of imagination. Associations like the Indian Space Exploration Association (ISRO) have exhibited India's capacities in space innovation, showing the way that the nation can try the impossible.

The development of Indian assembling greatness has been firmly connected to the visionary business people and business pioneers who have driven the way. People like Jamsetji Goodbye, the organizer behind the Goodbye Gathering, are commended for their spearheading commitments. Goodbye's inheritance stretches out past business; it incorporates the foundation of establishments like the Indian Organization of Science and Goodbye Foundation of Crucial Exploration, setting benchmarks for moral and economical strategic policies.

Dhirubhai Ambani, the organizer behind Dependence Businesses, is one more notable figure in India's assembling history. From unassuming starting points, he constructed a rambling .

1.1. Early Pioneers and Founding Principles

The beginning of Indian modern advancement were set apart by the spearheading endeavors of people who laid the foundation for the nation's assembling scene. These pioneers set up for modern advancement as well as laid out establishing rules that keep on molding India's financial and modern ethos.

Quite possibly of the earliest modern trailblazer in India was Jamsetji Nusserwanji Goodbye, frequently loved as the "Father of Indian Industry." In the late nineteenth hundred years, Jamsetji Goodbye imagined a modern renaissance that would change India's financial predetermination. He established the Goodbye Gathering, which would develop to become quite possibly of India's generally prestigious combination. Goodbye's vision reached out past simple business; it embraced the way of thinking of country building and cultural advancement.

Goodbye's modern endeavors included setting up material factories, laying out steel plants, and starting hydroelectric power projects. Strikingly, his highest accomplishment was the foundation of the Taj Mahal Royal residence in Mumbai, India's most memorable lavish inn, which filled in as a demonstration of his obligation to greatness and development. Also, Jamsetji Goodbye's vision stretched out to the formation of foundations like the Indian Establishment of Science in Bangalore and the Goodbye Organization of Major Exploration in Mumbai, planning to support logical schooling and examination in the country.

The establishing standards laid out by pioneers like Jamsetji Goodbye were established in moral strategic policies, a pledge to quality, development, and a feeling of social obligation. These standards established areas of strength for a point for future modern pioneers and organizations in India, setting elevated requirements for honesty, corporate administration, and local area government assistance.

Dhirubhai Ambani, one more notable figure in India's modern history, arose out of humble starting points to construct a domain through Dependence Ventures. Ambani's vision and enterprising soul prompted the fast extension of Dependence, at first in the petrochemical business and later in media communications, retail, and that's just the beginning. His tireless quest for progress and his capacity to adjust and enhance in a changing business climate procured him boundless acknowledgment.

The core values that Dhirubhai Ambani imparted in Dependence Ventures were well established in the way of thinking of offering some benefit to clients, engaging workers, and adding to the financial advancement of India. His accentuation on vertical joining and an emphasis on quality and cost-viability pushed Dependence Businesses to the cutting edge of Indian assembling.

These visionary business people were directed by rules that keep on reverberating in India's modern scene today. Their obligation to development, quality, and moral strategic policies laid the preparation for ensuing ages of modern pioneers, molding a culture of enterprising soul and flexibility.

The foundation of establishing standards wasn't restricted to individual business people however stretched out to the introduction of organizations and organizations that became inseparable from modern greatness in India. The Goodbye Gathering, established by Jamsetji Goodbye, typified a bunch of rules that stressed development, honesty, and social obligation.

Goodbye's accentuation on country building stretched out past business benefits to envelop a promise to local area government assistance and moral administration, which filled in as a guide for the whole modern area in the country.

Besides, the idea of public area endeavors (PSUs) in India assumed a critical part in molding the early modern scene. These administration possessed endeavors, laid out with the goal of advancing key ventures and diminishing reliance on imports, were directed by the standards of independence and monetary turn of events. They laid the preparation for modern extension and gave the establishment to India's assembling framework.

The Indian government's Five-Year Plans, started in 1951, additionally conveyed the soul of establishing standards. These plans expected to diagram the course for modern and monetary development in India. They set focuses for modern extension, focusing on areas like energy, transportation, and large equipment, advancing the standards of financial independence and arranged improvement.

The post-freedom period in India was portrayed by the quest for confidence and industrialization, epitomizing the establishing standards of monetary autonomy and social government assistance. The undertakings of early trailblazers and the foundation of core values were instrumental in forming the direction of India's modern development and monetary strategies.

As India progressed to a more changed economy during the 1990s, the scene of modern standards and practices started to move. The financial changes of 1991 presented another period of monetary advancement, opening up the Indian economy to worldwide exchange, unfamiliar ventures, and confidential area support. This shift saw a takeoff from the conventional state-controlled model towards a more market-situated approach.

The standards directing this new time of modern advancement were fixated on progression, privatization, and globalization. The center moved from protectionism to open business sectors, empowering rivalry, development, and proficiency in strategic approaches. The reception of these standards worked with the passage of private players into areas that were recently overwhelmed by state-claimed endeavors.

The Indian assembling area, specifically, saw a critical change with the reception of these new standards. Ventures like data innovation, cars, drugs, and materials encountered a flood in development and advancement. The advancement strategies cultivated a climate helpful for business and the development of new, unique players in the assembling field.

The rules that directed Indian assembling through this time were progressively impacted by ideas of worldwide seriousness, mechanical headway, and client driven techniques. Organizations expected to satisfy global guidelines of value, influence innovative progressions, and take special care of assorted client requests.

The data innovation (IT) area arose as a brilliant illustration of how these standards converted into progress. Indian IT organizations like Goodbye Consultancy Administrations (TCS), Infosys, and Wipro benefited from India's talented labor force and practical answers for take care of worldwide clients. These organizations zeroed in on development, quality, and consumer loyalty, laying out India as a worldwide center for IT administrations.

Also, the auto business embraced these standards, upgrading item quality, development, and plan to contend both locally and globally. Indian car producers like Goodbye Engines, Mahindra and Mahindra, and Maruti Suzuki took critical steps by embracing worldwide accepted procedures and client arranged systems.

The drug business, frequently perceived as the "Drug store of the World," likewise followed these standards by zeroing in on examination, advancement, and the development of reasonable conventional medications. Organizations like Dr. Reddy's

Research centers and Cipla earned worldwide respect by sticking to elevated expectations of value and advancement while giving reasonable medical services arrangements.

The rules that arose during the progression time underscored the significance of flexibility, development, and client driven approaches. Indian makers understood the meaning of fulfilling worldwide guidelines as well as fitting items and administrations to different client needs while keeping up with cost-effectiveness.

Besides, the 'Make in India' crusade, sent off in 2014, mirrored a re-visitation of standards supporting confidence, homegrown assembling, and a lift to monetary development. The drive planned to change India into a worldwide assembling center point, advancing native creation, improving simplicity of carrying on with work, and drawing in ventures. It revived the establishing standards of independence and financial strengthening, empowering development and business.

1.2. Shaping the Industrial Landscape

The development of India's modern scene has been an entrancing excursion that traverses hundreds of years. It is an account of change, variation, and development, with various powers and impacts molding the country's way to modern greatness. In this story, we investigate the powerful factors and verifiable setting that have added to the development of India's modern scene.

India's Modern Inheritance: A Verifiable Viewpoint

India's modern legacy is well established in its antiquated civic establishments, which were center points of development, craftsmanship, and exchange. The Indus Valley Progress, one of the world's most established metropolitan social orders, tracing all the way back to around 2500 BCE, established the groundwork for India's assembling custom.

Individuals of the Indus Valley were talented in metallurgy, stoneware, materials, and dot making, and they participated in broad exchange networks with far off areas. This early development's modern metropolitan preparation, waste frameworks, and art creation are characteristic of the country's antiquated modern ability.

The Mauryan and Gupta domains, which continued in the hundreds of years after the Indus Valley Development, made huge commitments to metallurgy and material assembling. These realms sustained the development of modern abilities and advances, bringing about astounding items and developments.

During the archaic period, India's assembling arrived at new levels, with the creation of fine materials like Muslin and Jamdani, desired in India as well as across the old Silk Street shipping lanes. The Mughal Domain, which governed a significant piece of India, further sustained the nation's assembling custom. Mughal rulers like Akbar the Incomparable were benefactors of human expression, supporting craftsmanship in materials, adornments, stoneware, and that's only the tip of the iceberg. Their support added to the prospering of different types of imaginative articulation and high level assembling strategies.

One of the most notable traditions of Mughal producing is the Taj Mahal, a magnum opus of design and imaginative greatness. The development of this catacomb encapsulates the complicated craftsmanship and scrupulousness that described Mughal producing. Talented craftsmans and skilled workers assumed a focal part in its creation, exhibiting the mix of structural designing and imaginative artfulness that undeniable the assembling greatness of the time.

The Frontier Time: Modern Change and Double-dealing

The frontier time frame, set apart by the appearance of the English East India Organization in the seventeenth 100 years, was a huge defining moment in India's modern scene. The English frontier rule significantly affected Indian culture, economy, and governmental issues, emphatically impacting the nation's assembling legacy.

The English provincial organization presented automation and current assembling strategies, which denoted the starting points of industrialization in India. This period saw the rise of material factories, shipbuilding, and the foundation of enterprises that depended on steam power and current apparatus. These advancements were the antecedents of India's cutting edge modern area.

In any case, the pioneer time was likewise portrayed by double-dealing, monetary channel, and arrangements that leaned toward English interests over those of the Indian subcontinent. English arrangements pointed toward extricating India's assets to support the provincial bosses, adding to monetary difficulties and deindustrialization.

The shady financial approaches of the English Raj incorporated the burden of weighty duties, land income frameworks that inclined toward property managers, and prejudicial exchange rehearses. India's native ventures and assembling customs were smothered, as the provincial rulers liked to import English made merchandise and materials, accordingly subverting the homegrown assembling area.

The frontier period featured the well established abuse that portrayed the connection among England and India. Monetary channel, inconsistent exchange rehearses, and the negligence for India's assembling capacities added to the financial difficulties that the nation confronted.

The Battle for Autonomy and the Introduction of Current Assembling

The battle for autonomy from provincial rule, which finished in India's hard-battled opportunity in 1947, denoted an essential stage in the country's set of experiences and its modern turn of events. The craving for independence and financial strengthening became key to the vision of a recently free India.

The post-freedom years were described by a change in center from agrarian and distinctive customs to industrialization. The initiative of the time perceived the need to construct an independent and industrialized country to meet the goals of individuals and defeated monetary difficulties.

One of the basic advancements during this period was the foundation of public area endeavors (PSUs). These administration claimed organizations were established to advance the improvement of key enterprises and lessen India's reliance on imports. The PSUs assumed a urgent part in areas like large equipment, steel creation, and foundation improvement.

The Indian government's Five-Year Plans, started in 1951, assumed a fundamental part in directing the nation's financial and modern development. These plans set focuses for modern turn of events, zeroing in on areas like energy, transportation, and large equipment. They were an impression of the standards of monetary independence and arranged financial turn of events.

The accentuation on "blended economy" standards, consolidating components of communism and free enterprise, advanced both state-claimed and confidential undertakings, looking for a harmony among public and confidential proprietorship. The blended economy model was pointed toward accomplishing impartial financial turn of events, supporting industrialization, and building an independent India.

The Standards of Modern Turn of events and Establishing Organizations

The rules that directed the modern advancement of the early post-autonomy time frame were established in independence, arranged improvement, and monetary strengthening. The accentuation on native modern development, upheld by open and confidential areas, established the groundwork for India's assembling foundation.

In addition, the standards directing this time stretched out to the foundation of key establishments. The Goodbye Gathering, established by Jamsetji Goodbye, embodied a bunch of rules that underscored development, respectability, and social obligation. The gathering's obligation to country building reached out past business benefits to envelop an obligation to the government assistance of the local area and moral initiative. The standards implanted in the Goodbye Gathering's DNA set exclusive requirements for uprightness, corporate administration, and cultural prosperity, filling in as a model for the whole modern area in India.

Furthermore, the idea of public area endeavors (PSUs) was instrumental in molding the early modern scene. These administration possessed endeavors were directed by standards of independence and monetary turn of events, fully intent on diminishing India's reliance on imported products and advancing homegrown assembling. They gave the establishment to modern extension and added to the improvement of key areas.

The Indian government's Five-Year Plans mirrored the standards of arranged monetary turn of events and independence. These plans set focuses for modern development, underscoring areas essential for the country's monetary turn of events, like energy, transportation, and large equipment. The standards of monetary independence and arranged development became fundamental to the country's modern turn of events.

The standards directing the early long periods of post-autonomy India zeroed in on independence, arranged improvement, and fair monetary development. The blend of public and confidential area cooperation, the advancement of native ventures, and the foundation of key organizations laid the basis for India's assembling framework and modern development.

The Shift towards Progression: New Standards for Another Period

The financial changes of 1991 introduced another time for India's modern scene, set apart by a critical takeoff from conventional monetary models. These changes, frequently alluded to as "advancement," pointed toward opening up India's economy to worldwide exchange, unfamiliar ventures, and confidential area investment. They addressed a change in outlook from protectionism to showcase situated monetary strategies.

The standards directing this new time were fixated on advancement, privatization, and globalization. India embraced these standards to encourage a climate helpful for business venture, development, and market-driven rehearses. The center moved from protectionism to open business sectors, empowering contest, mechanical headway, and productivity in strategic policies.

The advancement strategies changed India's modern scene, working with the passage of private players into areas that were recently overwhelmed by state-possessed undertakings. This shift permitted organizations to investigate new open doors, advance, and adjust to the changing monetary climate. The standards of contest, proficiency, and market-driven development became vital to India's modern turn of events.

The data innovation (IT) area was one of the huge recipients of these new standards. Indian IT organizations like Goodbye Consultancy Administrations (TCS), Infosys, and Wipro profited by India's talented labor force, capability in English, and practical answers for take special care of worldwide clients. These organizations zeroed in on development, quality, and consumer loyalty, laying out India as a worldwide center for IT administrations.

The auto business likewise embraced these standards, upgrading item quality, development, and plan to contend both locally and universally. Indian vehicle makers like Goodbye Engines, Mahindra and Mahindra.

1.3. Role in India's Economic Growth

India's financial development is a demonstration of the nation's persevering through flexibility and change in the worldwide scene. Fabricating, as an essential area of the economy, plays had a significant impact in forming India's financial direction. In this story, we dive into the multi-layered commitments of assembling to India's monetary development, investigating the area's authentic setting, contemporary importance, and future potential.

Verifiable Viewpoint: Assembling as a Monetary Support point

The verifiable meaning of assembling in India traces all the way back to its old civilizations, for example, the Indus Valley Human advancement, which flourished around 2500 BCE. These early social orders displayed progressed fabricating abilities in different areas, including metallurgy, earthenware, materials, and dot making. The Indus Valley individuals effectively partook in exchange organizations, sending out their products to far off districts, establishing the underpinnings of India's assembling legacy.

During the archaic period, India's assembling ability arrived at wonderful levels. The creation of fine materials like Muslin and Jamdani acquired global praise and became sought-after products along the antiquated Silk Street shipping lanes. The Mughal Realm further cultivated India's assembling greatness, with Mughal rulers like Akbar the Incomparable filling in as benefactors of artistic expression and specialties. The realm's help for craftsmanship in materials, gems, stoneware, and engineering added to the prospering of different types of creative articulation and high level assembling strategies.

The provincial time, set apart by English pioneer rule, achieved massive changes in India's assembling scene. The English presented automation and current assembling strategies, denoting the starting points of industrialization in the country. Material factories, shipbuilding, and ventures dependent on steam power and hardware arose during this period. While these advancements were the forerunners to India's cutting edge modern area, the frontier rule was likewise portrayed by double-dealing and financial arrangements that leaned toward English interests over those of the Indian subcontinent.

The post-freedom period denoted a change in India's concentration from agrarian and distinctive customs to industrialization. The country's initiative perceived the need to fabricate an independent and industrialized country, endeavoring to beat financial difficulties and meet the goals of its kin. Public area endeavors (PSUs) were laid out to advance the improvement of key enterprises and lessen India's dependence on imports. The public authority's Five-Year Plans, started in 1951, set focuses for modern development, focusing on areas like energy, transportation, and large equipment. The standards of independence and arranged financial improvement became key to India's modern advancement.

The Monetary Changes of 1991: A Change in perspective

The monetary changes of 1991 denoted a change in perspective in India's financial scene. These changes, frequently alluded to as "progression," expected to open up India's economy to worldwide exchange, unfamiliar speculations, and confidential area support. They addressed a takeoff from conventional monetary models, moving the concentration from protectionism to showcase situated financial strategies.

Progression presented standards of privatization, globalization, and contest, changing India's modern area. The approaches intended to cultivate a climate helpful for business venture, development, and market-driven rehearses. The reception of these standards worked with the passage of private players into areas that were recently overwhelmed by state-claimed endeavors.

The progression period significantly affected India's assembling scene. It released the innovative soul of the Indian people and empowered the development of businesses across different areas. Key areas of assembling, like data innovation (IT), cars, and drugs, encountered a flood in development and development.

The Data Innovation (IT) Transformation

One of the most groundbreaking advancements during the progression period was the development of the IT area in India. Indian IT organizations like Goodbye Consultancy Administrations (TCS), Infosys, and Wipro became worldwide forerunners in the arrangement of programming and IT administrations. These organizations gained by India's gifted labor force, capability in English, and savvy answers for serve worldwide clients. The standards of development, quality, and consumer loyalty became vital to the outcome of the Indian IT area.

The Indian IT industry's example of overcoming adversity epitomizes the job of assembling in monetary development. While IT administrations may not include customary assembling processes, the area contributed altogether to India's monetary turn of events. The development of the IT business made positions, created income, and supported India's standing as a worldwide center point for innovation and administrations.

The Car Insurgency

The car business was one more area that went through a huge change during the progression period. Indian auto makers, like Goodbye Engines, Mahindra and Mahindra, and Maruti Suzuki, extended their item portfolios, further developed item quality, and upgraded plan to contend both locally and globally. The business' emphasis on development, quality, and client situated methodologies made it an exceptional illustration of India's assembling greatness.

The progress of the Indian auto area assumed a significant part in India's financial development. It added to work creation, unfamiliar trade profit, and expanded interests in innovative work. The standards of worldwide seriousness and client driven approaches drove the area's advancement.

The Drug Business: The Drug store of the World

The drug business, frequently alluded to as the "Drug store of the World," is one more area that saw critical development during this period. Indian drug organizations became pioneers in the development of conventional medications, giving reasonable medical services arrangements not exclusively to the Indian populace yet in addition to the global market. Organizations like Dr. Reddy's Labs and Cipla acquired worldwide acknowledgment for their commitments to medical services.

The drug area's development was driven by standards of innovative work, quality, and moderateness. It added to India's monetary development by making position, producing trade income, and working with admittance to fundamental prescriptions.

The 'Make in India' Mission

The 'Make in India' crusade, sent off in 2014, addresses one more huge section in India's assembling story. This drive planned to change India into a worldwide assembling center point by advancing homegrown creation, upgrading simplicity of carrying on with work, and drawing in unfamiliar venture. The mission zeroed in on utilizing India's segment profit and various ability pool to reinforce producing across areas, from gadgets to protection hardware.

The 'Make in India' crusade built up the establishing standards of independence and homegrown assembling, further impelling India's financial development. It empowered business, development, and modern turn of events, with an emphasis on native creation and monetary independence.

The Change in Establishing Standards and Basic beliefs

The shift from independence and arranged financial development in the early post-freedom period to the standards of advancement, privatization, and globalization in the late twentieth century mirrored India's versatility and strength. The re-visitation of the establishing standards of confidence and homegrown assembling through the 'Make in India' crusade supported the obligation to financial development and advancement.

All through this excursion, certain fundamental beliefs stayed consistent. The obligation to advancement, quality, moral strategic approaches, and social obligation kept on forming India's assembling ethos. The standards of business venture, versatility, and client driven approaches assumed a significant part in cultivating modern greatness.

The Job of Assembling in Financial Development

Fabricating has been a foundation of India's financial development because of multiple factors:

Work Creation: Assembling areas, including IT, vehicles, and drugs, have been significant supporters of occupation creation in India. The development of these businesses has given business open doors to a critical piece of the labor force, adding to the country's monetary prosperity.

Trade Income: Assembling areas have essentially added to India's product income. Commodities of IT administrations, drugs, auto items, and other made merchandise have reinforced India's unfamiliar trade income, fortifying the country's financial situation on the worldwide stage.

Mechanical Progressions: Assembling has driven innovative headways and advancement. Organizations in the IT and car areas, for instance, have put resources into innovative work, prompting forward leaps in innovation and item quality.

Worldwide Seriousness: Assembling greatness in areas like IT and drugs has laid out India as a worldwide pioneer, improving the country's intensity on the global stage. Indian organizations have contended with and frequently beat worldwide partners, drawing in unfamiliar speculations and extending piece of the pie.

Monetary Broadening: The development of assembling has differentiated India's economy, decreasing its dependence on horticulture and giving a more adjusted financial design. This broadening has upgraded the country's flexibility to monetary changes.

Foundation Advancement: The extension of assembling ventures has driven framework improvement, including the development of modern zones, transportation organizations, and technology.

Chapter 2

Tata Group - A Century of Industrial Innovation

The Goodbye Gathering, an Indian worldwide combination, remains as a demonstration of 100 years of modern development that has molded the country's monetary scene. Established in 1868 by Jamsetji Goodbye, the gathering has developed into a force to be reckoned with across different enterprises, making a permanent imprint on India and the worldwide business world. This excursion of 100 years has been set apart by visionary authority, mechanical headways, and steadfast obligation to social obligation.

At its commencement, the Goodbye Gathering wandered into materials, an industry with promising development possibilities in provincial India. Under the sharp initiative of Jamsetji Goodbye, the gathering before long extended its tasks into steel, power, and neighborliness. One of the critical achievements in this excursion was the foundation of the Goodbye Iron and Steel Organization (TISCO), presently known as Goodbye Steel, in 1907. TISCO established the groundwork for the Indian steel industry, which has since become one of the biggest on the planet.

The modern vision of the Goodbye Gathering reached out past steel. Jamsetji Goodbye's obligation to country building was obvious when he started the development of the Taj Mahal Royal residence lodging in Mumbai in 1903. This lavish inn filled in as an image of plushness as well as turned into a demonstration of the gathering's obligation to giving top notch friendliness.

Throughout the long term, the Goodbye Gathering broadened its financial matters, venturing into areas like cars, synthetics, media communications, and data innovation. Goodbye Engines, for instance, arose as one of India's driving car makers, presenting notorious vehicles like the Goodbye Indica and the Goodbye Nano. This enhancement was an essential move that permitted the gathering to stay strong and versatile in a quickly changing worldwide market.

In the post-freedom time, the Goodbye Gathering proceeded to develop and improve. Goodbye Consultancy Administrations (TCS) was laid out in 1968, spearheading India's IT industry. Today, TCS is a worldwide forerunner in IT benefits and counseling, giving answers for clients around the world. The progress of TCS displayed the's gathering skill to perceive arising patterns and put resources into innovation driven endeavors.

The Goodbye Gathering's obligation to social obligation has been a center component of its character. Jamsetji Goodbye's confidence in rewarding society was obvious when he established the J.N. Goodbye Enrichment in 1892 to give grants to Indian understudies to concentrate abroad. This ethos of social obligation has gone on through the ages and has prompted the foundation of different charitable associations, including the Goodbye Trusts.

One of the most prominent commitments to society is the Goodbye Dedication Center, an incredibly famous malignant growth treatment and exploration organization. This organization plays had an essential impact in the battle against disease and has carried desire to endless patients. The gathering's emphasis on medical care additionally stretches out to Goodbye Wellbeing, which gives advanced medical services arrangements and telemedicine administrations.

The Goodbye Gathering's obligation to the climate and manageability is exemplified by Goodbye Power's endeavors in environmentally friendly power. The organization has put resources into wind and sunlight based power projects, adding to India's progress to spotless and environmentally friendly power energy sources. Furthermore, Goodbye Engines has been at the very front of creating electric vehicles, lining up with worldwide endeavors to battle environmental change.

The gathering's worldwide reach has extended throughout the long term, with Goodbye Consultancy Administrations (TCS) laying out areas of strength for an in various nations. TCS isn't just India's biggest IT administrations organization yet in addition one of the world's biggest, with a worldwide labor force and a client base that incorporates Fortune 500 organizations. This worldwide impression mirrors the Goodbye Gathering's versatility and capacity to contend on an overall scale.

The Goodbye Gathering's auto division, Goodbye Engines, has additionally made worldwide attacks. The procurement of Puma Land Meanderer (JLR) in 2008 was a huge achievement that brought famous English brands under the Goodbye umbrella.

JLR's prosperity under Goodbye possession features the gathering's obligation to supporting and upgrading its worldwide acquisitions.

The gathering's introduction to broadcast communications through Goodbye Correspondences plays had an essential impact in interfacing the world. The organization's undersea link organization and worldwide server farm presence have made it a vital participant in the broadcast communications industry, giving basic network foundation.

Goodbye Synthetic substances is another auxiliary that has extended its worldwide presence through acquisitions and key associations. The organization's mastery in synthetics and advancement has been instrumental in regions like farming and maintainability.

The Goodbye Gathering's obligation to development and exploration is obvious in its help of scholarly organizations. Goodbye Foundation of Major Exploration (TIFR) and Goodbye Establishment of Sociologies (TISS) are among the numerous instructive and research organizations that have gotten the gathering's support. These foundations have made critical commitments to the areas of science, innovation, and sociologies.

Goodbye's process has not been without its difficulties. Financial slumps, changing business sector elements, and worldwide rivalry have tried the gathering's versatility. In any case, the Goodbye Gathering's capacity to adjust and rethink itself has permitted it to defeat these difficulties.

A critical trial of the gathering's versatility was the 2008 worldwide monetary emergency. The obtaining of Panther Land Wanderer (JLR) only months before the emergency prompted critical monetary tensions. Goodbye Engines needed to explore through an intense time of declining deals and monetary rebuilding. In any case, the gathering's obligation to the drawn out capability of JLR and its readiness to put resources into innovative work permitted the English extravagance carmaker to bounce back and flourish.

Lately, Goodbye Gathering has gone through critical administration changes. The retirement of Ratan Goodbye, who filled in as the Executive of the gathering for more than twenty years, denoted a progress. Natarajan Chandrasekaran, a carefully prepared Goodbye veteran, succeeded him as Executive, introducing another time of initiative.

Chandrasekaran has kept on zeroing in on the gathering's basic beliefs of morals, trustworthiness, and social obligation. His initiative style has been portrayed by a guarantee to productivity, development, and supportability.

One of Chandrasekaran's key drives has been smoothing out the gathering's industry portfolio. This essential move expected to guarantee that each Goodbye organization works at top productivity and lines up with the gathering's guiding principle.

This interaction included selling non-center organizations and pulling together on areas where the Goodbye Gathering holds an upper hand.

The Goodbye Gathering's obligation to supportability and social obligation has stayed enduring. The gathering's drives, for example, Goodbye Water Mission, intend to give admittance to clean drinking water to underserved networks. Goodbye Trusts keep on working in regions like medical services, schooling, and provincial turn of events, contacting the existences of millions of individuals across India.

Goodbye Steel has likewise taken huge steps in decreasing its carbon impression and embracing manageable practices. The organization's obligation to ecological obligation remembers speculations for new innovations and cycles pointed toward diminishing emanations.

As the Goodbye Gathering enters its subsequent hundred years, it faces a quickly changing worldwide business scene. Innovation and development are driving disturbances across businesses, and the gathering should adjust to remain applicable. Goodbye Gathering's capacity to embrace computerized change and put resources into arising advances will be basic to its future achievement.

Goodbye Consultancy Administrations (TCS) has been at the front of advanced change, offering arrangements in regions like man-made consciousness, AI, and information examination. These capacities position TCS as a forerunner in assisting organizations with exploring the computerized age.

Goodbye Engines has additionally been investigating electric and independent vehicles, perceiving the moving elements in the auto business. The Goodbye Gathering's interest in Panther Land Meanderer (JLR) gives a potential chance to use JLR's aptitude in electric vehicles.

Goodbye Synthetic substances' advancements in manageable agribusiness and clean energy arrangements line up with the worldwide push for ecological manageability. The gathering's obligation to sustainable power, especially through Goodbye Power, is in accordance with the worldwide work to progress to cleaner wellsprings of force.

The Goodbye Gathering's proceeded with interest in innovative work, through organizations like Goodbye Exploration Advancement and Configuration Center (TRDDC), guarantees that it stays at the bleeding edge of mechanical development. These drives empower the gathering to remain ahead in regions like man-made consciousness, blockchain, and the Web of Things.

The gathering's initiative in the magnanimous area stays a center piece of its personality. The Goodbye Trusts keep on pursuing social turn of events, engaging networks, and tending to basic difficulties looked by India.

Drives like Goodbye Water Mission, which centers around giving clean water to underserved regions, highlight the gathering's obligation to social obligation.

The Goodbye Gathering's worldwide impression keeps on extending. Goodbye Consultancy Administrations (TCS) is available in north of 50 nations, and its worldwide labor force mirrors a different and comprehensive culture. TCS's worldwide arrive at positions it to give IT answers for clients across the world.

Goodbye Engines' procurement of Panther Land Wanderer (JLR) extended the gathering's presence in key worldwide business sectors. The progress of JLR under Goodbye possession is a demonstration of the's gathering skill to oversee and support worldwide acquisitions.

2.1. Historical Foundation

The idea of verifiable establishment is a basic part of figuring out the development of social orders and civic establishments over the long run. Verifiable establishments incorporate the thoughts, occasions, people, and conditions that have formed the course of mankind's set of experiences. These establishments act as the bedrock whereupon social orders fabricate their characters, values, organizations, and social stories. In this conversation, we will dive into the significance of verifiable establishments, investigate key models, and survey their persevering through importance in contemporary times.

Verifiable establishments are basically the structure blocks of a general public's past. They incorporate verifiable occasions, social practices, strict convictions, political turns of events, and monetary frameworks that have unfurled over hundreds of years. These establishments shape a general public's character and give a setting to grasping its current condition. By looking at the verifiable underpinning of a general public, we can acquire experiences into its qualities, customs, and how it has adjusted to different difficulties and changes since the beginning of time.

A basic verifiable starting point for some social orders is the idea of state development. The development of coordinated states and legislatures was a significant crossroads in mankind's set of experiences. It denoted the change from little, decentralized networks to bigger, more intricate social orders with laid out rules and organizations. Early human advancements like Mesopotamia, Egypt, and the Indus Valley laid the foundation for administration structures, general sets of laws, and social ordered progressions that keep on affecting current states.

Religion is another critical verifiable establishment that significantly affects social orders. Strict convictions and practices play had a focal impact in molding societies, virtues, and accepted practices. For instance, the spread of Christianity in Europe during the Medieval times affected craftsmanship, design, schooling, and the improvement of primitive social orders. Similarly, the ascent of Islam in the seventh century significantly molded the Middle Easterner world, presenting another overall set of laws and social request.

Monetary frameworks are essential verifiable establishments that have directed the manner in which social orders have coordinated their financial exercises. The change from agrarian economies to modern and post-modern economies, for example, was a groundbreaking verifiable shift. The Modern Upheaval in the eighteenth and nineteenth hundreds of years denoted a defining moment in monetary history, prompting urbanization, mechanical developments, and changes in labor rehearses. These financial changes keep on forming the cutting edge world.

The investigation and development of regions during the Period of Investigation in the fifteenth to seventeenth hundreds of years established the groundwork for the globalization of exchange and social trade. The trading of merchandise, thoughts, and innovations between the Old World and the New World prompted a mixing of societies and the spread of new yields, for example, maize and potatoes, which significantly affected worldwide weight control plans and farming practices.

Bondage and the transoceanic slave exchange address a dim and persevering through verifiable establishment that has had enduring results. The merciless oppression of African people groups by European powers and their constrained transportation to the Americas significantly affected the two sides of the Atlantic. The tradition of servitude is as yet felt today through issues connected with racial disparity, foundational prejudice, and the persevering through battle for social liberties and civil rights.

The verifiable underpinning of expansionism and dominion is one more essential part of world history. European provincial domains in Africa, Asia, and the Americas reshaped political limits, forced unknown dialects and societies, and took advantage of native people groups and assets. The repercussions of expansionism, including decolonization developments and post-provincial country building, keep on impacting worldwide international affairs.

The Illumination, a scholarly development in the seventeenth and eighteenth hundreds of years, denoted a significant change in mankind's set of experiences. It underscored reason, individual freedoms, and the quest for information. Illumination scholars like John Locke, Voltaire, and Jean-Jacques Rousseau added to the improvement of current political way of thinking, prompting the foundation of popularity based state run administrations and the assurance of common liberties.

The universal conflicts of the twentieth century were critical occasions that molded the course of history. The Second Great War and The Second Great War significantly affected worldwide governmental issues, prompting the foundation of worldwide associations like the Unified Countries and a guarantee to forestall further worldwide struggles. These conflicts likewise prompted the finish of realms and the redrawing of political limits in many areas of the planet.

In the domain of science and innovation, verifiable establishments are similarly significant. The Logical Upset of the sixteenth and seventeenth hundreds of years tested conventional convictions and added to the advancement of present day science. Advancements in fields like physical science, stargazing, and medication laid the foundation for mechanical headways that have changed society, from the creation of the steam motor to the improvement of the web.

The historical backdrop of social developments and upsets has likewise left an enduring verifiable establishment. The American Upset in the late eighteenth century prompted the foundation of the US as a vote based country, setting a model for future progressive developments all over the planet. The social equality development in the twentieth 100 years, exemplified by figures like Martin Luther Lord Jr., laid the basis for the battle against racial separation and isolation.

The effect of verifiable establishments isn't bound to a specific time or spot; rather, they keep on forming this present reality. The tradition of authentic occasions and thoughts should be visible in contemporary legislative issues, culture, and social designs. For example, the standards of a majority rules system, which rose up out of old Greece and the Edification, stay a directing power in current administration.

The tradition of expansionism and government is as yet apparent in the international elements of numerous locales. The limits of country states made during the frontier period have had enduring ramifications, frequently prompting clashes and difficulties connected with character and sway.

Strict convictions and practices keep on affecting people and social orders in different ways. The job of religion in molding virtues, normal practices, and clashes is a subject of continuous discussion and investigation.

The effect of bondage and the overseas slave exchange is felt in contemporary conversations on race, separation, and civil rights. Developments like People of color Matter and progressing banters about repayments are established in the authentic underpinning of subjection and its getting through outcomes.

Monetary frameworks, including private enterprise and communism, stay vital to contemporary discussions about abundance disparity, work freedoms, and the job of government in controlling business sectors. The worldwide economy is molded by authentic improvements like the Modern Unrest and the ascent of global organizations.

The continuous mission for common liberties and civil rights is profoundly associated with verifiable establishments. Developments for orientation balance, LGBTQ+ freedoms, and native privileges draw motivation from past battles for social equality and civil rights.

The effect of science and innovation is apparent in the computerized age, with the web and advances in fields like man-made brainpower, biotechnology, and space investigation. The Logical Transformation and ensuing logical progressions keep on molding how we might interpret the world and our capacity to advance.

2.2. Diverse Business Ventures

Various undertakings assume a fundamental part in the worldwide economy, mirroring the dynamic and consistently developing nature of business. Organizations today length an unbelievably wide range, enveloping different enterprises, plans of action, and inventive ways to deal with addressing the requirements of assorted client portions. This variety encourages financial development, work creation, and advancement. In this conversation, we will investigate the meaning of assorted undertakings, their effect on society, and the difficulties and amazing open doors they present.

The scene of assorted undertakings is huge and complex. These endeavors cut across different areas, including innovation, finance, medical care, retail, energy, and numerous others. They range from little new companies to worldwide partnerships, and they serve both nearby and worldwide business sectors. Every undertaking has a one of a kind incentive, plan of action, and interest group, mirroring the steadily developing requests of the cutting edge economy.

One of the essential drivers of different undertakings is advancement. In the present high speed world, advancement is fundamental for organizations to remain serious and pertinent. Business people and business pioneers consistently look for better approaches to tackle issues, work on existing items and administrations, or make altogether new ones. This drive for development has prompted a multiplication of new companies and creative plans of action, for example, membership based administrations, sharing economy stages, and online business arrangements.

The innovation area, specifically, has been a hotbed of development, with new businesses and laid out organizations pushing the limits of what is conceivable. Organizations like Apple, Google, and Amazon have changed enterprises and disturbed customary plans of action. Their advancements in cell phones, web search tools, and web based business have not just had an impact on the manner in which we live and work yet have additionally made huge monetary worth.

One more part of assorted undertakings is their capacity to make occupations and invigorate monetary development. Little and medium-sized endeavors (SMEs) are much of the time the foundation of economies, giving business open doors and adding to a country's Gross domestic product. In numerous nations, SMEs assume a significant part in driving development and serving neighborhood markets.

Globalization has likewise assumed an essential part in cultivating different undertakings. Propels in correspondence, transportation, and innovation have made it more straightforward for organizations to venture into global business sectors. Worldwide companies, with their different item contributions and worldwide presence, add to financial turn of events and significantly affect the worldwide inventory network.

Variety in undertakings isn't restricted to the items and administrations they offer yet additionally reaches out to their proprietorship and authority. The advancement of variety and consideration in the business world has acquired unmistakable quality, with additional organizations perceiving the worth of a different labor force. Variety in initiative and possession can prompt a more extensive scope of points of view, expanded development, and a superior comprehension of different client fragments.

The idea of assorted undertakings reaches out to the sorts of plans of action utilized. Conventional plans of action, for example, physical retail, are as yet common, however they coincide with current methodologies like internet business, membership administrations, and stage based organizations. These assorted plans of action reflect changing buyer inclinations and the quick digitization of the economy.

Online business, specifically, has seen colossal development and expansion. Organizations like Amazon, Alibaba, and eBay have changed retail as well as made huge biological systems where outsider merchants can contact worldwide crowds. The ascent of online commercial centers and advanced installment arrangements has empowered organizations to associate with clients in manners that were beforehand impossible.

The sharing economy, exemplified by organizations like Airbnb and Uber, addresses one more aspect of different undertakings. These stages work with distributed exchanges, permitting people to adapt their resources, whether it's their extra room, vehicle, or time. The sharing economy has disturbed conventional enterprises and presented inventive approaches to getting to administrations.

Membership based plans of action, predominant in businesses like media and diversion, have additionally acquired fame. Organizations like Netflix and Spotify offer on-request satisfied through month to month memberships, making repeating income streams and encouraging client devotion.

The variety of undertakings additionally stretches out to the medical care industry. Drug organizations, clinical gadget producers, and medical care suppliers are consistently growing new therapies, gadgets, and administrations to work on quiet consideration and results. Biotechnology new businesses are driving development in regions like genomics, customized medication, and regenerative treatments.

Clean energy and maintainability address one more area with different undertakings. As the world wrestles with natural difficulties and the need to progress to environmentally friendly power sources, organizations in sun oriented, wind, and other practical advancements are setting out open doors for development and ecological stewardship.

The monetary area is set apart by assorted undertakings, going from conventional banks and venture companies to fintech new businesses. Fintech organizations influence innovation to offer monetary types of assistance, for example, advanced installments, distributed loaning, and robo-consultants, disturbing conventional monetary establishments and extending admittance to monetary items.

New companies, specifically, assume a critical part in cultivating variety in undertakings. These arising organizations frequently challenge laid out players and acquaint inventive arrangements with longstanding issues. New companies flourish with the readiness and innovativeness of their pioneers and workers, and they add to work creation and financial development.

Nonetheless, various undertakings likewise face a scope of difficulties. Rivalry in the business world can be savage, and numerous new companies battle to acquire a traction on the lookout. Getting financing, exploring administrative obstacles, and building a client base are normal deterrents that business visionaries face.

The Coronavirus pandemic highlighted the weaknesses of assorted undertakings, especially private ventures. Lockdowns and limitations impacted areas like cordiality, retail, and travel, prompting monetary pain and terminations for some organizations. It stressed the significance of strength and versatility even with unanticipated difficulties.

Globalization and worldwide development, while offering amazing open doors, additionally present dangers. Political, financial, and social variables in various nations can confound market passage and business tasks. Worldwide partnerships should explore complex administrative conditions and international strains.

Various undertakings can add to pay imbalance on the off chance that not oversaw properly. Abberations in abundance and pay can broaden, especially when certain organizations or enterprises experience quick development, while others linger behind. Tending to these imbalances is a huge cultural test.

Online protection is a developing worry for organizations, all things considered. As computerized innovation turns out to be more fundamental to activities, the gamble of cyberattacks and information breaks increments. Organizations should put resources into powerful network safety measures to safeguard delicate information and client trust.

Natural maintainability is an issue that organizations should address. As worries about environmental change and asset shortage mount, organizations face strain to take on manageable practices and decrease their natural effect. Inability to do so can result in reputational harm and administrative outcomes.

Moral contemplations are likewise vital in the business world. Shoppers and financial backers progressively request straightforwardness, social obligation, and moral strategic policies. Organizations should wrestle with issues connected with work conditions, inventory network morals, and the effect of their items and administrations on society.

The developing idea of work presents difficulties and valuable open doors for different undertakings. The ascent of remote work, the gig economy, and robotization are reshaping the work market. Organizations should adjust to these progressions by encouraging an adaptable and talented labor force.

2.3. Global Impact and Leadership

Worldwide effect and authority are entwined parts of the cutting edge world, with countries, associations, and people assuming basic parts in forming the course of mankind's set of experiences. In a globalized and interconnected society, authority takes on new aspects, and the effect of choices and activities reverberates a long ways past public boundaries. In this conversation, we will investigate the ideas of worldwide effect and initiative, looking at their importance, challenges, and the pathways to accomplishing positive change on a worldwide scale.

Authority is a key power that shapes the world we live in. Initiative can emerge out of various sources, including public legislatures, global associations, worldwide partnerships, common society, and people. Compelling initiative impacts the heading of social orders, economies, and worldwide issues, making it an essential power for positive change.

Public authority assumes a focal part in forming a country's international strategy, worldwide relations, and commitments to worldwide issues. Country states have a special obligation to address the interests of their residents on the worldwide stage. Chosen authorities, ambassadors, and government organizations work to propel public goals while additionally teaming up with different countries to address normal difficulties, for example, environmental change, security, and general wellbeing.

Administration at the global level is exemplified by associations like the Assembled Countries (UN), the World Bank, the Worldwide Money related Asset (IMF), and local bodies like the European Association (EU) and the African Association (AU). These organizations give stages to collaboration, discretion, and advancement. The UN, specifically, fills in as a discussion for countries to resolve worldwide issues all in all and take a stab settled, common liberties, and economical turn of events.

Global enterprises employ huge impact in the present globalized world. These elements work across public limits, utilizing millions and creating significant income. Corporate pioneers pursue choices that influence their investors as well as the livelihoods of representatives, the climate, and the prosperity of networks where they work. Economical strategic policies and corporate social obligation have become fundamental to corporate authority.

Common society, enveloping non-legislative associations (NGOs), backing gatherings, and grassroots developments, assumes an imperative part in worldwide effect and administration. Common society entertainers frequently champion causes connected with basic freedoms, ecological insurance, general wellbeing, and civil rights. They consider states and enterprises responsible and advocate for positive change on issues like environment activity, admittance to schooling, and neediness decrease.

People can be strong specialists of worldwide effect and administration. Nobel laureates, activists, and powerhouses have utilized their foundation to cause to notice basic issues and rouse change. Unmistakable figures like Malala Yousafzai, Greta Thunberg, and Nelson Mandela have made permanent imprints on the worldwide stage, exhibiting the impact of individual authority.

Worldwide effect and authority stretch out past conventional limits and power structures. The interconnectedness of our reality has introduced another time where transnational issues, for example, environmental change, irresistible sicknesses, and network protection, require worldwide participation and authority. These difficulties require an aggregate methodology that rises above public interests and features the common predetermination of mankind.

The idea of worldwide authority includes both the obligation to address worldwide moves and the capacity to rouse, prepare, and coordinate global endeavors. Worldwide pioneers should explore complex international elements, cultivate coordinated effort, and show the moral and moral qualities important to successfully resolve worldwide issues.

The climate stands apart as perhaps of the most squeezing worldwide test. Environmental change, biodiversity misfortune, and contamination are issues that rise above borders and require bound together worldwide authority. The Paris Understanding, a global accord on environment activity, mirrors an aggregate obligation to relieving environmental change and its effects. It addresses a huge move toward worldwide initiative, as countries meet up to address a common ecological emergency.

Irresistible illnesses are another worldwide test that requests authority and participation. The Coronavirus pandemic highlighted the requirement for quick and facilitated global reactions to wellbeing emergencies. The World Wellbeing Association (WHO) assumed a focal part in directing the worldwide reaction, featuring the significance of global establishments in tending to general wellbeing crises.

Financial variations and neediness are likewise focal issues that require worldwide initiative. Global improvement objectives, like the Unified Countries' Supportable

Improvement Objectives (SDGs), give a system to tending to destitution, imbalance, and admittance to instruction and medical care. Multilateral associations like the World Bank work to diminish destitution and cultivate financial advancement in low- and center pay nations.

Basic freedoms are a major part of worldwide initiative. Pioneers and associations should advocate for the insurance of basic freedoms around the world, censuring separation, persecution, and viciousness. Worldwide pioneers play played urgent parts in propelling the reason for common freedoms, from the social liberties development in the US to the battle for orientation fairness.

Compromise and peacebuilding are essential regions for worldwide administration. Clashes, whether highway or intrastate, have decimating ramifications for social orders and require talented tact, intercession, and peacekeeping endeavors. The Assembled Countries and provincial bodies like the African Association experience been instrumental together as one arrangements and post-struggle remaking.

The worldwide reaction to general wellbeing emergencies is a demonstration of the significance of global collaboration and initiative. The Coronavirus pandemic, which arose in late 2019, spread quickly across borders, influencing individuals and economies around the world. Worldwide administration was fundamental in organizing reactions, sharing data, and creating immunizations and medicines.

Worldwide associations like the World Wellbeing Association (WHO) assumed a basic part in directing the worldwide reaction to the pandemic. The WHO gave direction on general wellbeing measures, led research, and composed endeavors to guarantee evenhanded admittance to immunizations and medicines. The cooperative endeavors of researchers, scientists, and medical services experts embody the potential for positive worldwide effect when pioneers and specialists cooperate.

With regards to environmental change, the Paris Understanding addresses a milestone in worldwide administration. The understanding, embraced in 2015, united essentially all nations to address the critical need to restrict a dangerous atmospheric devation. It incorporates responsibilities to lessen ozone depleting substance discharges, increment environment versatility, and offer monetary help to non-industrial countries. The Paris Understanding fills in as a model of worldwide participation and initiative notwithstanding an existential worldwide test.

Worldwide administration likewise incorporates strategy and compromise. The discussion and execution of nonaggression treaties, for example, the Dayton Accords that finished the Bosnian Conflict or the Great Friday Arrangement in Northern Ireland, exhibit the force of global strategy and administration in settling clashes and forestalling brutality.

Initiative in monetary turn of events and neediness decrease is a focal part of worldwide effect. Multilateral associations like the World Bank work with nations to advance practical monetary development, decrease destitution, and upgrade the prosperity of residents. The quest for the Unified Countries' Manageable Improvement Objectives

(SDGs) highlights the obligation to tending to neediness, disparity, and admittance to fundamental administrations like instruction and medical care on a worldwide scale.

Administration in the battle against segregation and mistreatment is exemplified by figures like Nelson Mandela, who assumed a vital part in finishing politically-sanctioned racial segregation in South Africa. Mandela's administration and promotion for compromise, common liberties, and correspondence act as a persevering through illustration of the potential for worldwide pioneers to drive positive change.

Worldwide effect and authority reach out to different spaces, like training, innovation, and social trade. Associations like UNESCO work to advance instructive open doors, safeguard social legacy, and work with diverse comprehension. Drives like the World Food Program battle craving and unhealthiness on a worldwide scale. Advancements in innovation, from the improvement of the web to the investigation of space, are driven by visionary pioneers and worldwide coordinated effort.

In spite of the positive capability of worldwide effect and authority, huge difficulties persevere. International pressures, philosophical partitions, and the quest for public interests can impede worldwide participation. The Assembled Countries, for instance, faces limits in addressing worldwide emergencies due to contending interests and blackball powers held by specific part states in the Security Board.

Natural difficulties, especially environmental change, keep on testing worldwide authority. While the Paris Understanding addresses an achievement in worldwide environment activity, the responsibilities made by nations are not generally adequate to meet the agreement's objectives. Accomplishing significant outflows decreases and tending with the impacts of environmental change stay huge difficulties.

Worldwide wellbeing emergencies, similar to the Coronavirus pandemic, uncover holes in worldwide authority and readiness. The reaction to the pandemic has been set apart by antibody dispersion abberations, absence of coordination.

Chapter 3

Mahindra Group - From Rural Beginnings to Global Domination

The Mahindra Gathering is a noticeable combination that embodies the excursion of a business from country starting points to worldwide control. Established in 1945 as a steel exchanging organization Ludhiana, India, by siblings J.C. Mahindra and K.C. Mahindra, the gathering has developed into a worldwide force to be reckoned with a presence in north of 100 nations across different areas, for example, auto, farming, aviation, data innovation, and monetary administrations. This change is a demonstration of the pioneering soul, versatility, and imaginative reasoning that describe the Mahindra Gathering.

The early long periods of the Mahindra Gathering were set apart by the difficulties of post-autonomy India. The organization's originators perceived the requirement for confidence and saw open doors in arising ventures. In 1947, they laid out an exchanging organization called Mahindra and Mohammed, which later became Mahindra and Mahindra.

A critical defining moment came in 1947 when India acquired freedom from English pioneer rule. The recently framed Indian government carried out financial arrangements that meant to advance independence and industrialization. The Mahindra siblings perceived the possible in this climate and left on their excursion of business.

The gathering's introduction to the auto area started with collecting Willys Jeeps in India, which were sought after because of their utility and rough terrain capacities. This try established the groundwork for Mahindra to turn into a main player in the Indian auto industry. Throughout the long term, the gathering's car division has made a different scope of vehicles, from rough jeeps to additional refined SUVs and electric vehicles. Mahindra's presence in the auto business isn't restricted to India; it has secured itself as a worldwide player, with a solid presence in a few global business sectors.

Notwithstanding cars, the Mahindra Gathering has a critical presence in the horticulture area. Perceiving the significance of horticulture in India's economy, the gathering presented the Mahindra Work vehicle in 1963, which turned into a distinct advantage for the Indian cultivating local area. The farm vehicle changed Indian horticulture as well as assumed a part in the Green Transformation by expanding rural efficiency.

Horticulture stays a basic area for the gathering, and it keeps on giving inventive answers for ranchers around the world. The Mahindra Gathering's obligation to rustic advancement is clear in its different drives, including giving admittance to current cultivating hardware, agritech arrangements, and enabling ranchers with information and assets to work on their vocations.

The gathering's worldwide development has been a vital element of its excursion from rustic starting points to worldwide mastery. Mahindra has utilized its ability in car and rural areas to universally extend its impression. Its presence traverses across the Americas, Europe, Asia, Africa, and Australia, with a solid spotlight on restricted assembling and dissemination.

The Mahindra Gathering's introduction to aviation and protection businesses mirrors its broadening and venture into high-innovation areas. Mahindra Aviation, laid out in 2008, centers around assembling airplane, parts, and administrations for the flight business. The gathering has likewise wandered into protection fabricating, delivering hardware and vehicles for military and paramilitary powers.

In the data innovation area, the Mahindra Gathering's IT administrations auxiliary, Tech Mahindra, has arisen as a worldwide player, giving programming administrations, counseling, and business process moving to clients across ventures. The organization's worldwide presence, development, and obligation to computerized change have made it a critical supporter of India's IT industry.

Monetary administrations comprise one more significant mainstay of the Mahindra Gathering's activities. Mahindra Money, the gathering's monetary administrations auxiliary, offers a scope of monetary items and administrations, including vehicle supporting, individual credits, and protection. It centers around provincial and semi-metropolitan business sectors, taking care of the monetary requirements of people and organizations here.

The Mahindra Gathering's obligation to social obligation and maintainability is obvious in its different drives, including Mahindra Ascend for Good, which centers around making positive change in the existences of individuals and networks. The collective endeavors' in the field of sustainable power, like breeze and sun oriented power, line up with worldwide drives to battle environmental change and advance clean energy.

The administration of the Mahindra Gathering has been instrumental in its development and achievement. Anand Mahindra, the ongoing Executive of the gathering, plays had a critical impact in forming its worldwide vision and system. His authority and vision have directed the gathering in its venture into new areas and markets.

One of the main attributes of the Mahindra Gathering's process is its obligation to advancement. The gathering has reliably embraced new innovations and patterns, from auto headways to computerized change. The quest for advancement is clear in the gathering's emphasis on electric vehicles (EVs) and supportability. Mahindra Electric, an auxiliary of the gathering, is devoted to creating and producing electric vehicles, adding to India's endeavors to diminish discharges and advance clean transportation.

Maintainability and ecological obligation have become focal subjects in the Mahindra Gathering's business tasks. The gathering is effectively associated with drives connected with supportable versatility, sustainable power, and ecological preservation. Mahindra's obligation to supportability lines up with worldwide endeavors to battle environmental change and advance a greener future.

The Mahindra Gathering's authority in corporate social obligation is reflected in drives, for example, the Mahindra Establishment, which upholds different social and local area advancement projects, including schooling, medical services, and ability improvement. The gathering's country and rural drives are pointed toward working on the existences of ranchers and networks through innovation and information sharing.

The excursion of the Mahindra Gathering from provincial starting points to worldwide control is a demonstration of the pioneering soul, flexibility, and inventive reasoning that describe the gathering. From a little steel exchanging organization post-freedom India, it has developed into a worldwide combination with a presence in different enterprises and markets. The gathering's obligation to country improvement, development, supportability, and social obligation sets a positive model for organizations around the world.

The Mahindra Gathering's different portfolio, spreading over businesses, for example, auto, agribusiness, aviation, IT, and monetary administrations, mirrors its capacity to adjust to changing business sector elements and embrace new open doors. Its worldwide impression is a consequence of key extension and limitation, permitting the gathering to take special care of the necessities of clients and networks in different districts.

The gathering's initiative, under the direction of Anand Mahindra, plays had a vital impact in forming its vision and worldwide methodology. His initiative style, portrayed by an emphasis on development, manageability, and social obligation, has situated the gathering as a worldwide forerunner in different areas.

As the Mahindra Gathering proceeds to develop and advance, it faces new difficulties and open doors. The worldwide business scene is set apart by fast mechanical progressions, changing purchaser inclinations, and advancing administrative conditions. The's ability to gather to adjust to these changes, advance, and stay focused on manageability and social obligation will decide its future achievement.

3.1. Origin and Growth

The idea of "beginning and development" is a central part of grasping the development of civilizations, social orders, associations, and thoughts over the entire course of time. It envelops the starting points of elements, thoughts, and developments, as well as their turn of events and change after some time. The investigation of beginning and development is crucial for acquiring experiences into the variables, occasions, and conditions that have molded the world as far as we might be concerned today. In this conversation, we will investigate the significance of grasping beginning and development, take a gander at key verifiable and contemporary models, and survey the getting through meaning of these ideas in the cutting edge world.

Beginning and development, with regards to mankind's set of experiences, is a multi-layered idea that incorporates the rise and improvement of different parts of human progress, from old social orders to present day associations. These viewpoints incorporate establishments, social practices, philosophies, and mechanical developments, among others.

The comprehension of beginning and development is central in understanding the elements of human social orders and their effect on the present. By inspecting the beginnings and resulting improvement of different components of human development, we can acquire a more profound enthusiasm for how they have molded the world we occupy today. Here are a few key regions where understanding beginning and development is of specific importance:

Civic establishments and Social orders: The investigation of the starting points and development of civic establishments and social orders assists us with understanding how human networks have advanced over the long haul. It uncovers the advancement of political frameworks, social progressive systems, financial designs, and social practices. For instance, the ascent of antiquated developments like Mesopotamia, Egypt, and the Indus Valley gives experiences into the underpinnings of administration, religion, and urbanization.

Foundations: The starting points and development of establishments, like states, general sets of laws, and instructive associations, are essential in figuring out their job in contemporary society. The advancement of popularity based administration, the development of overall sets of laws, and the foundation of instructive organizations have all added to the construction and working of current states.

Mechanical Headways: The historical backdrop of mechanical advancements, from the creation of the wheel to the computerized age, uncovers the advancement of human social orders and their effect on day to day existence. Understanding the beginning and development of advances like the print machine, the steam motor, and the web gives experiences into their extraordinary consequences for correspondence, transportation, and industry.

Philosophies and Conviction Frameworks: The beginning and development of philosophies, methods of reasoning, and strict convictions play had a significant impact in molding societies, values, and perspectives.

For instance, the advancement of Illumination thoughts in the seventeenth and eighteenth hundreds of years established the groundwork for present day political way of thinking, individual privileges, and the quest for information.

Financial Frameworks: The development and advancement of monetary frameworks, from agrarian economies to modern free enterprise, are fundamental for understanding how social orders have coordinated their financial exercises. The development of the Modern Upheaval in the eighteenth and nineteenth hundreds of years denoted a groundbreaking period in financial history, prompting urbanization, mechanical developments, and changes in labor rehearses.

Social Practices and Customs: Social practices, ceremonies, and customs have profound verifiable roots. The beginning and development of workmanship, music, writing, and different types of articulation mirror the qualities and character of social orders. For example, the Renaissance time frame in Europe saw the recovery of old style workmanship and picking up, prompting huge advancements in craftsmanship, culture, and scholarly idea.

Political Developments and Upsets: The beginnings and development of political developments and unrests, like the American Transformation and the social equality development in the US, lastingly affect the improvement of popularity based administration, social equality, and civil rights.

Logical Revelations and Advancements: The historical backdrop of logical disclosures and advancements, from the Copernican Transformation to the improvement of present day physical science and biotechnology, has reshaped how we might interpret the world and our capacity to develop.

Globalization: The beginnings and development of globalization, especially through the Time of Investigation in the fifteenth to seventeenth hundreds of years, significantly affect the trading of merchandise, thoughts, and advances between various regions of the planet. This globalization has formed societies, economies, and the interconnected idea of the advanced world.

Natural Changes and Manageability: Figuring out the starting points and development of natural difficulties, like deforestation, modern contamination, and environmental change, is fundamental for resolving contemporary issues connected with maintainability, asset protection, and biological prosperity.

Key Instances of Beginning and Development:

To acquire a more profound enthusiasm for the idea of beginning and development, we should investigate a few vital models from different spaces:

The Horticultural Upheaval: The change from hunting and assembling to settled farming denoted a huge beginning and development in mankind's set of experiences. This shift took into consideration the improvement of long-lasting settlements, the taming of plants and creatures, and the ascent of intricate social orders.

The Roman Domain: The beginnings of the Roman Republic and its resulting development into the tremendous Roman Realm impacted administration, regulation, and culture in the Western world. The Roman overall set of laws, design, and designing advancements keep on affecting contemporary society.

The Renaissance: The Renaissance, which began in Italy in the fourteenth hundred years, denoted a social and scholarly resurrection. It saw the resurgence of traditional learning, craftsmanship, and logical request, molding the advancement of present day Europe and then some.

The Modern Upheaval: The Modern Unrest, which started in the late eighteenth 100 years, addresses a groundbreaking period in mankind's set of experiences. It prompted the development of industrialization, urbanization, and mechanical headways, changing the idea of work, society, and the worldwide economy.

The Edification: The Illumination, a scholarly and philosophical development in the seventeenth and eighteenth hundreds of years, denoted the beginning and development of thoughts connected with reason, individual freedoms, and secularism. Its impact should be visible in the advancement of present day majority rule administration and common liberties.

The Data Age: The quick development of the Data Age, driven by the beginning of the web, has changed the manner in which individuals impart, access data, and lead business. It has reshaped businesses, economies, and social collaborations on a worldwide scale.

The Green Upheaval: The Green Upset, beginning during the twentieth 100 years, addresses a critical advancement in horticulture, with the development of high return crop assortments and worked on cultivating practices to address food security and yearning.

The Social equality Development: The beginning and development of the social liberties development in the US during the twentieth century prompted huge changes parents in law and cultural mentalities, propelling the reason for racial equity and civil rights.

The Advanced Upheaval: The Computerized Upset, portrayed by the beginning and development of computerized innovation, has reformed ventures like media communications, diversion, and medical care. It significantly affects the manner in which individuals work and connect.

The Natural Development: The beginnings and development of the ecological development, beginning during the twentieth hundred years, have brought issues to light about environmental issues and maintainability. It has prompted worldwide endeavors to address natural difficulties and moderate environmental change.

Meaning of Grasping Beginning and Development in the Advanced World:

The investigation of beginning and development remains exceptionally pertinent in the cutting edge world for a few convincing reasons:

Context oriented Understanding: Understanding the beginning and development of different parts of human progress gives significant setting to contemporary issues. It permits us to follow the verifiable underlying foundations of thoughts, organizations, and works on, assisting us with settling on informed choices and approaches.

Examples from History: The investigation of beginning and development offers significant illustrations from verifiable encounters, victories, and disappointments. By looking at previous occasions and their results, we can gain from the missteps and accomplishments of past ages.

Social and Verifiable Personality: Beginning and development are essential to social and authentic character. They assist networks and countries with laying out their remarkable stories, customs, and values. These stories add to a feeling of having a place and shared legacy.

Development and Progress: Understanding the beginnings of mechanical advancements and logical revelations can motivate contemporary advancement. The development and advancement of innovation and science can be utilized to address present and future difficulties.

Worldwide Interconnectedness: Beginning and development give bits of knowledge into the interconnected idea of the advanced world. The trading of thoughts, merchandise, and innovations between various locales of the world has added to globalization, accentuating the significance of worldwide participation and understanding.

Cultural Change and Progress: Inspecting the advancement of cultural standards, social liberties, and civil rights developments assists us with valuing the headway made and distinguish regions where further change is required.

Natural Mindfulness: The starting points and development of ecological difficulties feature the requirement for ecological mindfulness and manageable practices. It highlights the significance of resolving issues like environmental change and asset preservation.

3.2. Innovation and Sustainability

Development and maintainability are two principal points of support in tending to the squeezing difficulties within recent memory, as they hold the way to molding a superior and more prosperous future for humankind. These ideas are characteristically connected, as development gives the apparatuses and answers for drive manageability in our steadily advancing world. In this conversation, we will investigate the harmonious connection among development and manageability, their importance, and how they are entwined in resolving worldwide issues like environmental change, asset exhaustion, and ecological corruption.

Advancement, in its pith, addresses the most common way of making and applying novel thoughts, strategies, and innovations to achieve positive change. It is the impetus for progress, financial development, and cultural turn of events. The historical backdrop of human progress is set apart by earth shattering advancements that have changed each part of our lives, from the innovation of the wheel to the computerized insurgency of the 21st hundred years. Development isn't bound to mechanical progressions alone; it likewise includes new methodologies, plans of action, and techniques that upgrade proficiency, adequacy, and supportability.

Supportability, then again, is the idea of addressing the necessities of the present without compromising the capacity of people in the future to address their own issues. It spins around mindful asset the executives, natural protection, and even-handed financial turn of events. Supportability looks to find some kind of harmony between human prosperity, monetary development, and biological safeguarding. It is a reaction to the developing consciousness of the limited idea of our planet's assets and the hindering effect of unrestrained double-dealing.

The cooperative energy among development and manageability lies in their capability to address worldwide difficulties while encouraging financial thriving and social prosperity. Here are a few key regions where their interconnectedness is of principal significance:

Environmentally friendly power and Clean Innovations: Development plays had a critical impact in progressing environmentally friendly power sources, for example, sun oriented, wind, and hydroelectric power. These innovations give feasible options in contrast to non-renewable energy sources, moderating the unfriendly impacts of environmental change. Economical energy developments diminish ozone depleting substance outflows and reduction reliance on limited petroleum product saves.

Round Economy: The idea of a round economy advances the development of economical practices where assets are utilized, reused, and reused in a shut circle. Developments in reusing, squander decrease, and material proficiency limit natural effects and add to long haul maintainability by lessening waste and saving assets.

Green Transportation: Development in green transportation incorporates electric vehicles (EVs), mixture advancements, and elective energizes. These improvements decline discharges and diminish the ecological effect of transportation frameworks, adding to the supportability of metropolitan versatility and decreasing air contamination.

Brilliant Agribusiness: Agrarian development is significant for reasonable food creation. Progressions in accuracy agribusiness, biotechnology, and supportable cultivating rehearses advance harvest yields, diminish asset wastage, and limit the ecological impression of food creation.

Water The board: Maintainable water the executives depends on advancement to address difficulties like water shortage and tainting. Innovations for productive water system, wastewater treatment, and water protection assist with guaranteeing a feasible stockpile of clean water for momentum and people in the future.

Reasonable Materials: Advancements in materials science have prompted the improvement of manageable and eco-accommodating materials, for example, bioplastics, practical materials, and low-carbon building materials. These developments decrease the natural effect of creation and utilization.

Metropolitan Preparation and Plan: Manageable metropolitan preparation and plan developments intend to make more decent and harmless to the ecosystem urban areas. Highlights like green framework, productive public transportation, and metropolitan cultivating add to decreased contamination, energy utilization, and upgraded personal satisfaction for metropolitan occupants.

Asset Effectiveness: The enhancement of asset use is vital to maintainability. Developments in asset effective advancements, like energy-productive apparatuses and eco-accommodating assembling processes, limit squander and decrease asset utilization.

Preservation and Biodiversity: Imaginative ways to deal with preservation and biodiversity safeguarding assist with safeguarding biological systems, untamed life, and normal living spaces. These drives assume a critical part in guaranteeing the drawn out soundness of the planet's biodiversity.

Social and Financial Consideration: Reasonable advancement incorporates endeavors to advance social and monetary consideration. Developments in monetary consideration, microfinance, and social business venture empower financial development that helps a more extensive fragment of the populace.

The worldwide test of environmental change represents the basic interchange among development and manageability. Environmental change is an immediate result of human exercises, principally the consuming of petroleum derivatives and deforestation. To address this emergency, creative arrangements are fundamental. The improvement of environmentally friendly power innovations, like sunlight based chargers and wind turbines, addresses a fantastic move toward diminishing ozone depleting substance outflows and changing to a practical energy future.

Advancement is additionally vital in carbon catch and capacity innovations, which plan to alleviate the effect of past discharges. Also, brilliant matrix advances improve energy productivity, while electric vehicles and maintainable transportation arrangements decrease outflows in the transportation area.

Supportability is similarly significant in the battle against environmental change. Reasonable practices, for example, reforestation and preservation of regular living spaces, assist with sequestering carbon and safeguard biodiversity. Economical land use arranging can decrease deforestation, and maintainable farming practices limit outflows and safeguard soil wellbeing.

Development in information examination and environment displaying adds to how we might interpret environment designs and empowers more precise expectations. This information is fundamental for informed navigation and successful environment approaches. Economical structure works on, including green development materials and energy-effective plans, decrease emanations from the development and activity of structures.

The cooperation among advancement and maintainability reaches out to the business world too. Organizations perceive that supportability is as of now not simply a question of moral obligation however a basic part of long haul achievement. Organizations are progressively incorporating supportability into their procedures, not exclusively to decrease natural effect yet in addition to improve seriousness and productivity.

For instance, organizations are taking on manageability driven developments, for example, eco-accommodating bundling, store network enhancement, and carbon bookkeeping frameworks. They are additionally perceiving the significance of corporate social obligation and moral strategic approaches. Developments here can prompt expense investment funds, expanded client unwaveringness, and a positive effect on the organization's standing.

Moreover, maintainable practices and inventive innovations can open up new business sectors and income streams. The perfect energy area, for example, has seen critical development and occupation creation. Feasible items and administrations, from natural food sources to energy-proficient machines, take special care of a developing customer interest for eco-cognizant decisions.

The convergence of advancement and manageability is especially obvious in the field of economical money. Imaginative monetary items, for example, green bonds and effect financial planning, channel capital into ventures and drives that add to supportability. These monetary instruments produce returns as well as help drives like environmentally friendly power projects, reasonable horticulture, and clean water access.

Reasonable money likewise advances straightforwardness and responsibility in business activities. Organizations that take on supportable practices are progressively expected to uncover their natural, social, and administration (ESG) execution. This straightforwardness empowers financial backers to pursue informed choices and dispense cash-flow to ventures that line up with their qualities and maintainability objectives.

With regards to economical turn of events, developments in friendly business and microfinance have enabled people and networks to address social and ecological difficulties. These drives center around practical answers for destitution, disparity, and ecological debasement. By giving admittance to monetary assets and backing, they empower networks to foster imaginative and maintainable answers for nearby issues.

The Unified Countries' Practical Improvement Objectives (SDGs) address a worldwide obligation to address probably the most squeezing difficulties within recent memory. Development assumes a focal part in accomplishing these objectives. The SDGs envelop goals connected with destitution decrease, wellbeing, schooling, orientation correspondence, clean water, reasonable and clean energy, industry and framework, diminished disparities, mindful utilization and creation, and environment activity, among others.

Advancement and innovation are instrumental in propelling these objectives. For instance, versatile financial arrangements have empowered monetary consideration, diminishing neediness and cultivating monetary development. Telemedicine and e-learning stages have stretched out medical care and instruction to underserved networks. Economical agribusiness rehearses have further developed food security and diminished ailing health.

3.3. Expansion into Diverse Sectors

The venture into different areas is an essential move that many organizations, associations, and combinations embrace to broaden their business portfolios, relieve dangers, and tap into new income streams. This approach is in many cases driven by a craving for development, flexibility in an evolving market, and the quest for cooperative energies between various areas. In this conversation, we will investigate the meaning of venture into different areas, take a gander at key verifiable and contemporary models, and evaluate the advantages and difficulties related with this procedure.

Venturing into assorted areas includes wandering past an association's center abilities or essential industry to investigate open doors in various business sectors or enterprises. This essential expansion is spurred by a few variables:

Risk Relief: Depending entirely on one industry or market can make an association defenseless against financial changes and market-explicit dangers. Enhancement spreads risk across different areas, diminishing an association's reliance on a solitary income source.

Income Development: Venturing into different areas can prompt expanded income streams, permitting an association to develop and flourish. Various areas frequently have unmistakable client bases and income cycles, giving extra roads to pay.

Collaborations and Strategically pitching: A few associations find cooperative energies between their center business and new areas they enter. This collaboration takes into consideration strategically pitching amazing open doors and the making of significant worth added administrations.

Flexibility: Expansion empowers an association to adjust to changing economic situations and customer requests. At the point when one area faces difficulties, an enhanced organization can turn toward additional promising areas.

Advancement: Investigating different areas can animate advancement as associations bring new thoughts and points of view starting with one industry then onto the next, prompting the improvement of new items or administrations.

Upper hand: Entering different areas can give an association an upper hand by giving a more extensive scope of contributions contrasted with contenders with additional restricted portfolios.

Authentic Instances of Venture into Assorted Areas:

General Electric (GE): GE's venture into different areas is a notable verifiable model. At first, GE was centered around electrical apparatuses and power age. Over the long run, it enhanced into aeronautics, medical services, money, and that's only the tip of the iceberg. This enhancement assisted GE with turning into a worldwide modern combination.

Virgin Gathering: Richard Branson's Virgin Gathering is one more illustration of an organization that effectively ventured into different areas. It started as a record mark however developed to incorporate carriers, media communications, wellbeing, and space investigation. The Virgin brand is presently inseparable from different ventures.

Siemens: Siemens, established as a message maker, ventured into areas like medical care, energy, transportation, and modern mechanization. Its different arrangement of items and administrations takes special care of different enterprises.

Berkshire Hathaway: Warren Buffett's Berkshire Hathaway has put resources into a large number of areas, including protection, utilities, customer products, and innovation. The organization's enhanced possessions have added to its prosperity and life span.

Samsung: Samsung, initially an exchanging organization, ventured into different areas, including gadgets, shipbuilding, and development. The combination's gadgets division, specifically, has turned into a worldwide pioneer.

Contemporary Instances of Venture into Assorted Areas:

Amazon: Amazon, at first an internet based book shop, has ventured into assorted areas, including online business, distributed computing (Amazon Web Administrations), amusement (Amazon Prime), and man-made consciousness (Alexa).

Letter set Inc.: The parent organization of Google, Letter set has wandered into assorted areas past pursuit and publicizing. Its auxiliaries incorporate Waymo (self-driving vehicles), Verily (life sciences), and Calico (biotechnology).

Tencent: Tencent, initially known for its informing application WeChat, has ventured into gaming, online entertainment, web based business, and monetary innovation. The organization's different portfolio has made it a worldwide tech goliath.

Tesla: While Tesla is famous for its electric vehicles, it has expanded into energy capacity (Tesla Powerwall) and sun oriented innovation (SolarCity securing), intending to give practical energy arrangements.

Walmart: Walmart, a retail goliath, has ventured into web based business and innovation through acquisitions like Jet.com and Flipkart. The organization means to contend with online retailers and tech organizations.

Advantages of Venture into Different Areas:

Risk Relief: Enhancement diminishes an association's openness to takes a chance in a solitary area. Monetary slumps, market changes, or area explicit difficulties have a lesser effect when an organization works in different enterprises.

Income Development: By entering new areas, associations can take advantage of extra income streams, possibly helping their monetary exhibition and empowering them to jump all over development chances.

Strategically pitching Potential open doors: Organizations with different portfolios can use collaborations between areas, strategically pitching items or administrations to a more extensive client base. This prompts expanded deals and client dependability.

Flexibility: Various area development improves an association's capacity to adjust to changing economic situations. In the event that one area encounters challenges, the organization can turn to other additional promising areas.

Development: Expansion encourages advancement by carrying new points of view starting with one industry then onto the next. This cross-fertilization of thoughts can prompt the improvement of new, noteworthy items or administrations.

Upper hand: Working in various areas can give an organization a strategic advantage by offering a more extensive scope of contributions contrasted with contenders that spend significant time in just a single area.

Worldwide Development: Expansion can empower an organization to grow its worldwide presence. Entering different areas can open ways to new global business sectors and open doors.

Difficulties of Venture into Different Areas:

Asset Allotment: Broadening requires critical asset designation, including capital, faculty, and time. Associations should cautiously deal with these assets to guarantee outcome in numerous areas.

The executives Intricacy: Dealing with a different arrangement of organizations can be perplexing. Various areas have unmistakable prerequisites, and successful administration is vital to organize activities.

Coordination Issues: Blending assorted areas might present difficulties concerning combination. Crisscrossed societies, innovations, or plans of action can impede collaboration and effectiveness.

Cutthroat Elements: Venturing into new areas frequently implies going up against laid out players. This opposition can be wild, requiring significant exertion and assets to acquire a traction.

Administrative Consistence: Various areas are dependent upon different guidelines and consistence necessities. Exploring these legitimate and administrative scenes can interest.

Brand and Notoriety Dangers: Disappointment in one area can adversely affect an association's image and notoriety across all areas. Keeping areas of strength for an is essential while differentiating.

Monetary Dangers: Expansion might bring about monetary strain on the off chance that not oversaw as expected. Working in various areas can open an association to monetary dangers that should be painstakingly checked.

Absence of Mastery: Associations might come up short on important skill to succeed in specific areas. Gaining or fostering the expected abilities is in many cases fundamental for progress.

Market Timing: Entering new areas brilliantly is critical. Misconstruing market timing can bring about botched open doors or passage into areas that are as of now soaked.

Arrangement with Basic beliefs: Enhancement ought to line up with an association's guiding principle and long haul goals. Entering areas that are incongruent with an association's main goal can prompt vital misalignment.

Chapter 4

Reliance Industries - Transforming India's Textile and More

Dependence Enterprises, a combination with its underlying foundations profoundly implanted in India's modern scene, has gone through an exceptional change throughout the long term. Established by Dhirubhai Ambani in 1966, Dependence started as a material assembling organization in an unassuming community in Gujarat. From that point forward, it has developed into a worldwide force to be reckoned with, assuming a crucial part in molding India's financial scene. This paper investigates the excursion of Dependence Enterprises, zeroing in on its change from a material organization to a multi-layered combination, and its critical commitments to India's modern and monetary development.

Dependence Enterprises' process started in the clamoring town of Naroda, where Dhirubhai Ambani began a little material organization called Vimal during the 1960s. Around then, India's material industry was divided, with obsolete hardware and an absence of present day innovation. Dhirubhai's vision was clear: he expected to change the Indian material area by utilizing state of the art innovation, effective assembling processes, and a sharp feeling of business intuition.

In the underlying years, Dependence confronted a few difficulties, including furious rivalry, capital requirements, and administrative obstacles. Be that as it may, Dhirubhai's dauntless soul and inventive systems assisted the organization with conquering these obstructions.

He zeroed in on vertical reconciliation, which implied that Dependence would control each part of the material assembling process, from obtaining unrefined components to delivering completed items. This upward joining technique worked on functional effectiveness as well as decreased costs altogether.

Dependence's development in the material business was set apart by the foundation of its most memorable plant in Naroda in 1966. The organization's item range extended to incorporate a wide assortment of manufactured materials, like polyester and nylon. These developments permitted Dependence to offer top notch items at cutthroat costs, quickly acquiring piece of the pie and laying out areas of strength for a presence in the Indian material industry.

By the last part of the 1970s, Dependence had become one of the main material makers in India, and its items were exceptionally pursued in homegrown and worldwide business sectors. Dhirubhai's forceful way to deal with extension saw the organization expanding into different areas, including petrochemicals, refining, and media communications. This essential move established the groundwork for Dependence's change from a material organization into a differentiated combination.

The petrochemicals business denoted a huge defining moment for Dependence. In 1985, the organization set up a top notch petrochemical plant in Hazira, Gujarat. This was an intense move, as it was an area distant from its material beginnings. Notwithstanding, this expansion ended up being a masterstroke. The Hazira plant turned into the foundation of Dependence's development and outcome in the petrochemical area. It not just delivered many items, including polymers, synthetic substances, and intermediates yet in addition empowered the organization to take advantage of new product markets.

As Dependence kept on extending, it perceived the significance of making a solid and proficient production network. The organization put vigorously in framework, including the development of India's first and biggest confidential area port at Jamnagar, Gujarat. This port, known as Dependence Petrol's Jamnagar Treatment facility, assumed an imperative part in improving the organization's operations capacities and decreasing transportation costs.

The refining area likewise saw an essential crossroads in Dependence's set of experiences with the charging of the Jamnagar Treatment facility in 1999. This mammoth venture turned into the world's biggest grassroots processing plant and was a demonstration of the organization's obligation to pushing the limits of innovation and scale. The Jamnagar Treatment facility not just supported India's independence in refined oil based goods yet in addition changed Dependence into a worldwide player in the oil and gas industry.

One of the surprising parts of Dependence's process was its capacity to draw in worldwide associations and ventures. In 2000, Dependence framed an essential collusion with the world's biggest oil organization, ExxonMobil, to upgrade its petrochemical business.

This association made ready for innovative progressions, information sharing, and admittance to worldwide business sectors.

Dependence Businesses likewise extended its presence in the broadcast communications area. In 2002, it sent off Dependence Infocomm, which later became Dependence Correspondences. This noticeable the organization's introduction to the universe of broadcast communications, giving a great many administrations, including versatile and fixed-line communication, broadband, and computerized TV. The telecom area in India was profoundly cutthroat, yet Dependence's aggressive techniques and ventures assisted it with cutting a critical specialty here.

Dependence's commitment to India's media communications upset couldn't possibly be more significant. The send off of Jio, its telecom auxiliary, in 2016 denoted a game-changing second in the business. Jio's troublesome passage was portrayed by offering high velocity 4G web at super reasonable costs. This prompted a sensational expansion in web entrance and openness the nation over. A huge number of Indians who were recently barred from the computerized age were unexpectedly associated, and the information utilization in India soar. Jio's effect on computerized consideration and the ascent of the advanced economy in India has been significant.

The outcome of Jio's 4G administrations was joined by a forceful rollout of fiber optic broadband administrations across India, further reinforcing Dependence's presence in the advanced space. Yet again furthermore, Jio's aggressive designs for the sending of 5G innovation in India vowed to reform the broadcast communications area.

Past broadcast communications, Dependence made key acquisitions in different areas, including retail. The obtaining of famous corporate store like Hamleys, Dependence Retail's organization with worldwide goliaths like Amazon, and its forceful extension in the coordinated retail space highlighted the organization's obligation to turning into a critical player in the retail business.

Dependence's retail arm, Dependence Retail Adventures, sent off JioMart, a web based business stage, to gain by the developing pattern of internet shopping. This drive intended to coordinate neighborhood supermarkets and little retailers into the computerized biological system, guaranteeing that they profited from the internet business blast, instead of being abandoned. JioMart's imaginative methodology resounded with customers, offering a large number of items and home conveyance administrations. It tried to consolidate the accommodation of internet shopping with the trust and commonality of neighborhood retail.

Dependence Enterprises additionally wandered into the environmentally friendly power area, perceiving the significance of supportable turn of events. The organization declared its obligation to turn into a net carbon-impartial venture by 2035. This aggressive objective included huge interests in efficient power energy projects, including sunlight based and wind power age.

The change towards cleaner and more reasonable energy sources was a demonstration of Dependence's obligation to ecological obligation and adjusting its strategic policies to worldwide environment objectives.

Dependence's commitments to India's monetary development have been significant. The organization's interests in different areas, including producing, broadcast communications, retail, and energy, have created huge work amazing open doors. Additionally, its obligation to mechanical development and advanced consideration has pushed India into the computerized age, making it quite possibly of the quickest developing computerized economy on the planet.

The Jamnagar Treatment facility, frequently alluded to as the "Processing plant to the World," assumed a pivotal part in decreasing India's reliance on oil imports and reinforcing its energy security. This gigantic complex had a refining limit of over 1.2 million barrels each day, making it the biggest on the planet. It handled different sorts of raw petroleum, including weighty and acrid rough, which permitted India to expand its wellsprings of raw petroleum and decrease its weakness to supply interruptions.

Dependence's effect on India's modern scene reached out to the energy area. The organization put vigorously in oil and gas investigation and creation, adding to India's energy independence.

4.1. Rise of Reliance Industries

The ascent of Dependence Enterprises is an exceptional excursion that mirrors the dynamism and versatility of India's corporate scene. Laid out in 1966 by Dhirubhai Ambani, Dependence started as a humble material assembling organization in Naroda, Gujarat. From these modest beginnings, it changed into a rambling combination with a different portfolio spreading over petrochemicals, refining, media communications, retail, and environmentally friendly power.

Dependence's initial years were set apart by Dhirubhai Ambani's resolute vision and creative business techniques. The material business in India during that period was portrayed by discontinuity, obsolete apparatus, and restricted mechanical progressions. Dhirubhai perceived the huge potential in patching up this area. His methodology was two-overlay: to modernize and streamline the material assembling processes and to guarantee vertical joining by controlling each part of the creation cycle.

The technique of vertical incorporation, a sign of Dependence's initial development, involved the organization's command over the whole worth chain, from unrefined substance obtaining to the creation of completed materials. This approach upgraded functional effectiveness as well as fundamentally scaled down costs, permitting Dependence to offer top notch items at cutthroat costs. Thusly, the organization quickly acquired piece of the pie and started laying out major areas of strength for an in the Indian material industry.

The 1970s and 1980s saw a progression of huge achievements for Dependence. It left on an excursion of enhancement into petrochemicals, refining, and media communications. The expansion technique was instrumental in reshaping Dependence from a material driven organization into a complex combination.

The petrochemical area assumed a critical part in this change. In 1985, Dependence set up a cutting edge petrochemical plant in Hazira, Gujarat. This essential move denoted a takeoff from materials however was driven by the organization's central goal to differentiate its portfolio and grow its span. The Hazira plant turned into a foundation of Dependence's outcome in the petrochemical area, delivering a wide exhibit of items, including polymers, synthetics, and intermediates. It served the homegrown market as well as worked with the organization's entrance into global business sectors.

The material business' tradition of vertical reconciliation tracked down a characteristic expansion in the petrochemical area. With an emphasis on innovation and development, Dependence situated itself as a forerunner in the creation of engineered filaments, plastics, and synthetic substances. This enhancement filled in as a defensive measure against financial slumps, lessening the organization's dependence on a solitary area.

Dependence perceived from the beginning that a strong inventory network and foundation are crucial to its development. The organization put altogether in foundation advancement, finishing in the development of India's most memorable confidential area port at Jamnagar, Gujarat. This port, known as the Jamnagar Treatment facility, turned into an indispensable part of Dependence Oil's tasks, upgrading strategic abilities and decreasing transportation costs.

The venture into the refining area denoted one more groundbreaking crossroads in Dependence's set of experiences. In 1999, the organization authorized the Jamnagar Processing plant, the world's biggest grassroots treatment facility at that point. This task was an accomplishment of designing and innovation as well as a demonstration of the organization's obligation to pushing the limits of scale and productivity. The Jamnagar Treatment facility assumed a crucial part in India's independence in refined oil based goods, hence reinforcing Dependence's situation as a worldwide player in the oil and gas industry.

Dependence's ability for drawing in worldwide organizations and speculations became apparent with its coordinated effort with ExxonMobil in 2000. This coalition was instrumental in upgrading the organization's petrochemical business, considering innovation trade and admittance to worldwide business sectors. It exhibited Dependence's capacity to explore the intricacies of worldwide business and lay out productive joint efforts.

Dependence's expansion stretched out to the media communications area in 2002 when it sent off Dependence Infocomm, which later advanced into Dependence Correspondences.

This move addressed the organization's entrance into the dynamic and exceptionally serious telecom industry. Dependence Interchanges offered a large number of administrations, including portable and fixed-line communication, broadband, and computerized TV.

While the telecom area in India was furiously cutthroat, Dependence's aggressive techniques and ventures permitted it to cut out a huge presence. The organization's commitments to India's broadcast communications upheaval were groundbreaking. In 2016, Dependence Jio, its telecom auxiliary, presented rapid 4G internet providers at extraordinarily reasonable costs. This problematic section prompted a significant expansion in web entrance and openness all through India, interfacing a large number of individuals who were recently prohibited from the computerized age.

Jio's effect on advanced consideration and the quick development of the computerized economy in India was significant. The drive changed the manner in which individuals got to data as well as catalyzed the advancement of new computerized administrations, applications, and online business stages. India's web scene turned into a fruitful ground for development and business.

The progress of Jio's 4G administrations was supplemented by a forceful rollout of fiber optic broadband administrations across India, further reinforcing Dependence's traction in the computerized space. Jio's aggressive designs for the organization of 5G innovation in India vowed to alter the telecom area by and by, making way for future development and computerized change.

Past media communications, Dependence wandered into the retail area through essential acquisitions and associations. The obtaining of notable corporate store like Hamleys, alongside organizations with worldwide goliaths like Amazon, highlighted the organization's obligation to laying out a huge presence in the retail business. Dependence Retail Adventures, the retail arm of the aggregate, sent off JioMart, an internet business stage that planned to combine the accommodation of web based shopping with the trust and commonality of nearby retail. The stage's creative methodology resounded with purchasers, offering a large number of items and home conveyance administrations.

Dependence's commitments to India's financial development have been significant. The organization's interests in different areas, including fabricating, media communications, retail, and energy, have created critical work amazing open doors, straightforwardly and by implication. Also, its obligation to mechanical advancement and computerized consideration has moved India into the computerized age, making it perhaps of the quickest developing computerized economy on the planet.

The Jamnagar Treatment facility, frequently alluded to as the "Treatment facility to the World," assumed a critical part in decreasing India's reliance on oil imports and reinforcing its energy security. With a refining limit of over 1.2 million barrels each day, it was the biggest on the planet, handling different sorts of unrefined petroleum, including weighty and sharp rough.

This variety in unrefined handling permitted India to differentiate its wellsprings of raw petroleum and decrease its weakness to supply disturbances.

Dependence's effect on India's modern scene reached out to the energy area. The organization put vigorously in oil and gas investigation and creation, adding to India's energy independence. The revelation of the KG-D6 gas fields in the Krishna Godavari Bowl was a huge accomplishment and reinforced the country's petroleum gas holds. It exemplified Dependence's obligation to India's energy security and confidence.

The sustainable power area arose as another wilderness for Dependence. In a time where maintainability and natural obligation became fundamental, the organization reported its desire to turn into a net carbon-impartial endeavor by 2035. This elaborate significant interests in environmentally friendly power projects, including sun based and wind power age. The progress toward cleaner and more economical energy sources exhibited Dependence's obligation to adjusting its strategic approaches to worldwide environment objectives and lessening its ecological impression.

4.2. Textile Manufacturing Excellence

Material assembling greatness is a subject that envelops the workmanship and study of creating materials - an imperative and fundamental industry with profound verifiable roots. Materials are not simply textures; they are woven into the texture of our regular routines, filling in as a fundamental part of dress, goods, and modern applications. In this exposition, we dig into the universe of material assembling, investigating the development, mechanical headways, and the basic job it plays in economies and social orders around the world.

The historical backdrop of material assembling is a story of human resourcefulness. From the earliest long periods of human progress, individuals have been turning, winding around, and coloring strands to make textures for dress and asylum. Archeological proof uncovers that materials were created as far back as 6000 BC. Old civilizations, like the Egyptians, Greeks, and Romans, had deep rooted material enterprises, creating textures from materials like flax, fleece, and silk. These early material cycles laid the basis for the future improvement of material assembling.

The creation of the turning wheel in the Medieval times denoted a huge jump in material assembling. It took into account the automated creation of yarn, which was recently finished manually, expanding the proficiency and consistency of material creation. Creations like the turning jenny and the power loom during the Modern Transformation in the late eighteenth century further upset the business, prompting an enormous expansion in material creation limit.

The development of material assembling took one more goliath jump with the approach of the cotton gin in the mid nineteenth hundred years. Eli Whitney's innovation fundamentally decreased the time and work expected to isolate cotton filaments from their seeds, making cotton a more suitable and practical choice for material creation. This development assumed a significant part in the development of the material business in the US and all over the planet.

As the material business kept on developing, advancements in transportation and correspondence assumed a fundamental part in its extension. The advancement of the steam motor and the extension of rail lines empowered the development of unrefined substances, completed items, and gifted work, working with the development of material assembling communities. Moreover, the message considered better coordination and correspondence between various phases of the material inventory network.

The material business experienced massive changes during the twentieth hundred years, including the improvement of engineered filaments. In 1935, Wallace Carothers, a scientific expert at DuPont, created nylon, the main manufactured fiber. This leading edge opened up additional opportunities for material assembling, as engineered filaments offered sturdiness, flexibility, and a great many applications. After some time, other engineered filaments like polyester, acrylic, and spandex were grown, further extending the material business' capacities.

In the last 50% of the twentieth 100 years, material assembling saw the reception of mechanization and computerization. These innovative progressions considered more exact command over the assembling system, prompting expanded quality and consistency. PC supported plan (computer aided design) and PC helped fabricating (CAM) frameworks changed how materials were planned and created. These frameworks further developed effectiveness as well as decreased the lead time from plan to creation.

The globalization of material assembling has been a characterizing element of the 21st 100 years. Makers started to source materials and work from different regions of the planet, looking for cost investment funds and admittance to particular skill. This globalization has made complicated and interconnected supply chains that stretch across borders, making it vital for material producers to deal with their procedure on a worldwide scale.

Today, material assembling greatness includes a perplexing transaction of innovation, development, and supportability. Present day material assembling offices are furnished with best in class apparatus, considering elevated degrees of computerization and accuracy. Advanced mechanics and man-made consciousness have found their direction into material assembling processes, from slicing and sewing to quality control and bundling.

Notwithstanding mechanical progressions, manageability has turned into a critical worry in the material business. The natural effect of material assembling, from water and energy utilization to waste and contamination, has prompted a developing accentuation on eco-accommodating practices. Feasible material assembling centers around lessening water utilization, utilizing eco-accommodating colors and synthetic substances, and limiting waste through reusing and upcycling endeavors.

One of the essential difficulties in material assembling is obtaining economical unrefined components. Cotton, for example, is a broadly utilized regular fiber, yet its development can have critical ecological effects.

Hereditarily altered cotton and natural cultivating rehearses are two methodologies utilized to make cotton development more manageable. Furthermore, endeavors are in progress to foster maintainable options in contrast to customary materials, for example, textures produced using bamboo, hemp, and reused materials.

Endeavors to work on the functioning circumstances and social effect of material assembling have built up forward movement as of late. Associations and certificates, like Fair Exchange and the Worldwide Natural Material Norm (GOTS), plan to guarantee that material creation is completed under moral and socially mindful circumstances. These drives center around fair wages, safe workplaces, and the preclusion of kid work in the material business.

As far as mechanical headways, the ascent of computerization and savvy fabricating in material manufacturing plants is molding the eventual fate of the business.

Robotization, using robots and high level hardware, has smoothed out many cycles, from texture slicing and sewing to quality control and bundling. These advances further develop effectiveness as well as upgrade item quality and consistency.

Savvy fabricating, frequently alluded to as Industry 4.0, includes the coordination of information examination, the Web of Things (IoT), and man-made brainpower into the assembling system. This permits makers to screen and upgrade creation continuously. Sensors and information investigation can foresee gear disappointments, lessen margin time, and limit energy utilization, making material assembling more proficient and practical.

One more key pattern in material assembling is the ascent of 3D printing. While 3D printing has been principally connected with enterprises like aviation and medical services, it is making advances into material creation. 3D printing offers the capacity to make complex and tweaked material designs, altering plan prospects and the creation of elite execution textures.

Supportability stays a focal worry in material assembling. The business is tending to natural difficulties by taking on eco-accommodating practices. The material area drinks critical measures of water and energy and creates significant waste. To alleviate these natural effects, material makers are investigating elective coloring and completing techniques, like waterless coloring advancements and the utilization of biodegradable or non-harmful synthetic substances.

Round design is one more idea getting forward movement in the material business. This approach centers around making materials that can be reused and reused, lessening how much attire that winds up in landfills. Material makers are exploring different avenues regarding imaginative materials that can be handily reused or changed into new items. Furthermore, many organizations are creating reclaim programs, where purchasers can return old dress and materials for reusing or upcycling.

Advancements in materials are likewise molding the material business' future. Biomanufacture, which includes developing materials from living creatures like microscopic organisms and growths, is a quickly arising field. These economical materials offer the possibility to change the material business by diminishing the requirement for asset serious cycles and engineered strands.

Nanotechnology is one more area of interest in material assembling. Nano-sized particles can be implanted in materials to improve their properties, for example, making them more strong, water-repellent, or antimicrobial. These headways open up additional opportunities for making materials with improved execution attributes.

Material assembling greatness is something other than the development of texture; it envelops the whole inventory network, from unrefined substance obtaining to completed item conveyance. A productive and maintainable store network is basic to the progress of material assembling. The store network incorporates processes like material obtaining, turning, winding around or weaving, coloring and getting done, and quality control.

Material makers source unrefined components like cotton, fleece, silk, and manufactured strands from different districts, contingent upon the particular requirements of their items. The quality and attributes of these materials impact the last texture's properties, like surface, strength, and variety. The obtaining of supportable and morally created natural substances has turned into a need for some makers.

Turning is the method involved with changing crude filaments into yarn, which is the structure block of texture. Current turning factories are furnished with modern hardware that can create an extensive variety of yarn types, from fine and fragile strings to hearty and rock solid ones.

Winding around and sewing are the two essential strategies used to transform yarn into texture. Winding around includes intertwining yarns to make an organized and stable texture, while weaving produces a more adaptable and stretchy texture. The decision among winding around and sewing relies upon the planned .

4.3. Diversification into Petrochemicals, Refining, and Telecommunications

Dependence Ventures' noteworthy excursion from a material assembling organization to a broadened combination is a demonstration of visionary initiative, vital development, and a tireless quest for greatness. The organization's venture into petrochemicals, refining, and broadcast communications stamped essential crossroads in its set of experiences and reshaped India's modern scene.

The Enhancement Drive

Dependence Businesses perceived the requirement for broadening to relieve gambles related with overreliance on a solitary industry. The material business, while once the foundation of the organization, was wrestling with difficulties like worldwide rivalry and changing buyer inclinations. The requirement for broadening drove Dependence to investigate new areas with development potential.

Petrochemicals: A Foundation of Development

The petrochemical area arose as a characteristic decision for enhancement. In 1985, Dependence Enterprises charged a best in class petrochemical plant in Hazira, Gujarat. This undeniable an essential shift from materials to a high-development and mechanically progressed area. The Hazira plant created an extensive variety of petrochemical items, including polymers, synthetic substances, and intermediates, serving both homegrown and worldwide business sectors.

The outcome of Dependence in the petrochemical business was ascribed to its attention on innovation and advancement. The organization utilized its center assets in assembling and functional greatness to arise as a forerunner in the development of manufactured filaments, plastics, and synthetic substances. This enhancement added to Dependence's income as well as gone about as a defensive measure against financial slumps in the material business.

Vertical Reconciliation: A Critical System

Dependence's way to deal with vertical coordination, which was a sign of its progress in materials, tracked down a characteristic expansion in the petrochemical area. The organization meant to control each part of the creation cycle, from obtaining unrefined components to assembling completed items. This approach improved functional productivity and altogether decreased costs, making Dependence items exceptionally serious on the lookout.

The Jamnagar Processing plant: A Unique advantage

In 1999, Dependence Ventures dispatched the Jamnagar Processing plant, which was a weighty task and the world's biggest grassroots treatment facility at that point. The processing plant, situated in Jamnagar, Gujarat, was a demonstration of Dependence's obligation to pushing the limits of innovation, scale, and proficiency. It had a refining limit of over 1.2 million barrels each day, which fundamentally supported India's independence in refined oil based goods.

One of the distinctive highlights of the Jamnagar Treatment facility was its capacity to deal with different kinds of unrefined petroleum, including weighty and sharp rough. This expansion in rough handling permitted India to diminish its weakness to supply disturbances and enhance its wellsprings of raw petroleum. Dependence's capacity to handle these various kinds of raw petroleum further reinforced its situation as a worldwide player in the oil and gas industry.

Worldwide Joint efforts

Dependence Enterprises' capacity to draw in global organizations and speculations became apparent with its coordinated effort with ExxonMobil in 2000. The essential union expected to upgrade the organization's petrochemical business. It worked with innovation trade, information sharing, and admittance to worldwide business sectors. This cooperation was instrumental in driving mechanical progressions in the petrochemical area.

Dependence kept on investigating worldwide organizations and acquisitions as a feature of its development technique. The organization's forceful methodology and eagerness to team up with industry monsters highlighted its desire to assume a huge part in the worldwide energy and synthetic compounds scene.

Broadcast communications: An Intense Jump

While the petrochemical area denoted Dependence's broadening into industry fragments lined up with its center assets, the move into media communications was a takeoff from its conventional concentration. In 2002, Dependence sent off Dependence Infocomm, which later developed into Dependence Correspondences. This noticeable the organization's entrance into the profoundly aggressive media communications industry.

Dependence Interchanges offered many administrations, including versatile and fixed-line communication, broadband, and advanced TV. The telecom business in India was furiously cutthroat, with a few laid out players. Notwithstanding, Dependence's aggressive techniques and significant speculations permitted it to cut out a critical specialty here.

The Telecom Transformation

Dependence's commitments to India's media communications upheaval couldn't possibly be more significant. In 2016, the organization presented Jio, its telecom auxiliary, which upset the business by offering high velocity 4G internet providers at particularly reasonable costs. This move was a distinct advantage, as it prompted a significant expansion in web entrance and openness the nation over.

The effect of Jio's 4G administrations on advanced incorporation was significant. A great many Indians who were recently barred from the computerized age were out of nowhere associated. This fast expansion in web openness changed the manner in which individuals got to data, correspondence, and amusement. It additionally catalyzed the development of the advanced economy in India, making the country perhaps of the quickest developing computerized economy on the planet.

Jio's Aggressive Plans

Jio's prosperity was not restricted to 4G administrations. Once more the organization had aggressive designs for the sending of 5G innovation in India, which vowed to upset the media communications area. The boundless reception of 5G innovation would open up additional opportunities for fast web, ongoing information transmission, and the Web of Things (IoT).

The rollout of fiber optic broadband administrations was one more huge improvement in Jio's excursion. This forceful extension intended to give rapid web availability to homes and organizations across India. By offering an exhaustive set-up of computerized administrations and foundation, Jio situated itself as a one-stop objective for every single advanced need.

Enhancement into Retail

Notwithstanding petrochemicals, refining, and media communications, Dependence Enterprises wandered into the retail area, showing its obligation to enhancement and extension. The procurement of famous corporate store like Hamleys and associations with worldwide web based business monsters like Amazon featured the organization's desires in the retail business.

Dependence Retail Adventures, the retail arm of the aggregate, sent off JioMart, an internet business stage pointed toward blending the comfort of web based shopping with the trust and commonality of neighborhood retail. JioMart's inventive methodology looked to associate neighborhood supermarkets and little retailers to the advanced biological system, guaranteeing that they profited from the online business blast.

Manageable Practices and Efficient power Energy

Dependence Ventures perceived the significance of maintainability and ecological obligation. The organization made critical interests in the environmentally friendly power area, adjusting its strategic approaches to worldwide environment objectives. In 2021, Dependence Ventures reported its obligation to turn into a net carbon-unbiased endeavor by 2035.

The change to cleaner and more reasonable energy sources included interests in efficient power energy projects, including sun based and wind power age. These drives meant to diminish the organization's carbon impression and add to an all the more ecologically mindful future. Dependence's obligation to maintainability mirrored its affirmation of the pressing need to address environmental change and natural preservation.

The Excursion Towards Round Design

Maintainability endeavors reached out to the design and materials industry, where Dependence Businesses tried to advance roundabout style. Roundabout style is a methodology that spotlights on making materials that can be reused, reused, or reconsidered, lessening how much dress that winds up in landfills.

Endeavors were made to foster imaginative materials that could be effortlessly reused or changed into new items. Furthermore, reclaim programs were presented, permitting shoppers to return old attire and materials for reusing or upcycling. These drives expected to decrease the ecological effect of the design business and advance mindful utilization.

Dependence Enterprises' commitments to India's monetary development have been critical. The organization's interests in different areas, including fabricating, media communications, retail, and energy, have created work potential open doors straightforwardly and in a roundabout way.

Its obligation to mechanical development and computerized incorporation has moved India into the advanced age, making it one of the quickest developing advanced economies internationally.

Dependence Businesses' commitment to the petrochemical area has fortified India's situation as a worldwide player in the business. The Jamnagar Treatment facility, frequently alluded to as the "Treatment facility to the World," assumed a urgent part in decreasing India's reliance on oil imports and supporting its energy security.

The organization's interests in oil and gas investigation and creation have added to India's energy independence. The revelation of the KG-D6 gas fields in the Krishna Godavari Bowl altogether added to the country's flammable gas holds, lessening its dependence on exorbitant imports and upgrading energy security.

In the environmentally friendly power area, Dependence Enterprises' obligation to efficient power energy projects addresses a positive move toward natural maintainability. By embracing sustainable power sources like sun based and wind power, the organization has decreased its carbon impression as well as added to India's change to cleaner and more feasible energy sources.

Chapter 5

Sun Pharmaceutical - The Pillar of India's Pharma Industry

Sun Drug Ventures, established in 1983 by Dilip Shanghvi, has arisen as a transcending presence in India's drug industry. The organization's excursion from an unobtrusive startup to becoming one of the world's biggest and most regarded drug firms is a demonstration of its vision, devotion to quality, and immovable obligation to medical care. Sun Pharma's ascent has been set apart by a progression of key acquisitions, a persistent spotlight on innovative work, and a worldwide impression that reaches out across mainlands. In this exposition, we will dive into the advancement of Sun Drug Businesses, its effect on India's pharma area, and its commitments to worldwide medical services.

Establishment and Early Development

Sun Pharma's initiation can be followed back to 1983, when Dilip Shanghvi, a youthful business visionary, chose to wander into the drug business. Around then, the Indian drug scene was portrayed by a couple of laid out players, and section hindrances were high. By the by, Shanghvi's aspiration and vital reasoning drove him to distinguish open doors in the business.

Sun Pharma at first began as a maker of mental medications, cutting out a specialty for itself in an exceptionally specific fragment. The organization's initial spotlight on quality and advancement established the groundwork for its future achievement. It put resources into cutting edge fabricating offices and rigid quality control situation, making way for its excursion towards turning into a drug force to be reckoned with.

One of the key rules that directed Sun Pharma's development was the accentuation on innovative work (Research and development). The organization perceived the significance of fostering its own protected innovation and making an arrangement of separated items. This obligation to Research and development would separate Sun Pharma and drive its mission for greatness.

Key Acquisitions: The Defining moment

In the last part of the 1990s and mid 2000s, Sun Pharma set out on a progression of key acquisitions that would end up being critical in its development direction. The obtaining of Caraco Drugs in the US in 1997 checked Sun Pharma's entrance into the worldwide market. This move extended its impression as well as given admittance to an exceptionally directed and quality-cognizant market.

The securing of Ranbaxy Research facilities in 2014 was a milestone crossroads in the organization's set of experiences. Ranbaxy, at that point, was quite possibly of India's biggest drug organization. The arrangement shot Sun Pharma to the place of the biggest drug organization in India and one of the top generics producers on the planet. It likewise carried with it a broad item portfolio, producing capacities, and a huge presence in developing business sectors.

The incorporation of Ranbaxy into Sun Pharma was a perplexing interaction that included smoothing out tasks, settling administrative issues, and guaranteeing a smooth change for the two organizations' representatives and partners. Sun Pharma's capacity to effectively explore these difficulties exhibited its administration's sharpness and its obligation to maintaining the best principles.

Worldwide Impression and Administrative Consistence

Sun Pharma's extension wasn't restricted to India and the US. The organization has consistently expanded its presence in different worldwide business sectors, including Europe, Japan, and arising economies. These extensions were driven by an essential spotlight on administrative consistence, quality confirmation, and the presentation of creative items.

In the European market, Sun Pharma laid out areas of strength for a through the securing of a few organizations, like Taro Drugs in the US and certain organizations of Novartis in Japan. These moves empowered the organization to get to new business sectors, influence laid out circulation organizations, and fortify its item portfolio.

The accentuation on administrative consistence and quality confirmation assumed an essential part in Sun Pharma's worldwide extension. The organization's commitment to sticking to the rigid prerequisites of administrative offices in various areas has assisted form with trusting and validity. It has put vigorously in strong quality control measures, best in class fabricating offices, and a hearty store network to guarantee that its items fulfill the most noteworthy worldwide guidelines.

Innovative work: The Foundation of Advancement

Sun Pharma's obligation to innovative work is a foundation of its development and development. The organization has reliably contributed a huge piece of its incomes in Research and development exercises. This devotion to logical examination and development has prompted the improvement of a strong item pipeline.

Sun Pharma's Research and development endeavors include a great many helpful regions, from dermatology and ophthalmology to nervous system science and cardiology. The organization's researchers and specialists work enthusiastically to find and foster new medications, details, and conveyance frameworks. This emphasis on development has brought about a hearty protected innovation portfolio, with various licenses and brand names to its name.

A prominent illustration of Sun Pharma's obligation to development is its work in specialty drugs. The organization has created and sent off perplexing and separated items, like inward breath items and biosimilars, which require modern innovation and ability. These undertakings have extended Sun Pharma's piece of the pie as well as emphatically influenced patient consideration by giving admittance to cutting edge treatment choices.

Worldwide Effect and Commitment to Medical services

Sun Pharma's effect reaches out a long ways past its corporate victories. It assumes a crucial part in tending to worldwide medical care difficulties, especially in the space of moderateness and admittance to quality meds. The organization's broad arrangement of conventional medications, biosimilars, and specialty drugs offers savvy options in contrast to marked prescriptions, making medical services more available to a large number of patients around the world.

The presentation of nonexclusive medications by Sun Pharma has been instrumental in decreasing medical services costs and expanding admittance to fundamental meds. By and large, the accessibility of these generics has cut down the costs of medications essentially, helping patients and medical care frameworks. The organization's consistent endeavors to create and popularize great generics decidedly affect general wellbeing.

Sun Pharma's introduction to biosimilars, which are bioequivalent adaptations of biologic medications, can possibly change treatment choices for complex illnesses. Biosimilars are in many cases more reasonable than their biologic partners, making progressed treatments open to a more extensive populace. Sun Pharma's biosimilar portfolio, covering regions like oncology and immunology, addresses a critical commitment to medical services around the world.

In specialty drugs, Sun Pharma has presented creative medicines for conditions like psoriasis, epilepsy, and visual sicknesses. These therapies upgrade patient consideration as well as proposition special remedial choices for complex ailments.

Corporate Obligation and Maintainability

Sun Pharma perceives the significance of corporate obligation and maintainability. The organization is focused on moral strategic approaches, straightforwardness, and great administration. It sticks to severe quality and security guidelines, guaranteeing the wellbeing and prosperity of its workers and the networks wherein it works.

Maintainability is a center part of Sun Pharma's corporate system. The organization is aware of its natural effect and is effectively attempting to diminish its carbon impression. Drives like energy preservation, squander the executives, and mindful water utilization are vital to its manageability endeavors. Sun Pharma likewise upholds social and local area government assistance programs that emphasis on medical services, schooling, and ability improvement.

Difficulties and Future Possibilities

While Sun Pharma's process has been portrayed by various accomplishments and achievements, it has not been without its portion of difficulties. The drug business is profoundly aggressive and dependent upon rigid administrative oversight. Evaluating pressures, expanding contest, and developing medical care strategies in various areas present continuous difficulties.

Following these difficulties, Sun Pharma proceeds to adjust and advance. The organization's strength and capacity to explore the intricate scene of the drug business are characteristic of its obligation to long haul supportability and development. Sun Pharma's essential enhancement, interest in Research and development, and world-wide extension position it well for what's to come.

What's to come possibilities for Sun Pharma seem promising. The organization's obligation to advancement and the improvement of perplexing generics, biosimilars, and specialty drugs are supposed to drive development. The rising pervasiveness of constant illnesses and the interest for cutting edge medicines give huge open doors to the organization to have a beneficial outcome on medical services.

Sun Pharma's venture into computerized wellbeing and telemedicine is one more sign of its ground breaking approach. The organization's interests in advanced medical services stages and telehealth administrations mirror its obligation to upgrading patient consideration, openness, and accommodation.

5.1. Pharmaceutical Landscape in India

The drug scene in India is a dynamic and multi-layered area that has gone through momentous change throughout the long term. India has arisen as one of the world's biggest drug makers and exporters, providing reasonable medications to nations across the globe. This article dives into the advancement of the drug business in India, its commitments to worldwide medical services, challenges it faces, and the manner in which forward in this always developing scene.

Verifiable Viewpoint

The foundations of India's drug industry can be followed back to old Ayurvedic and Unani medication rehearses. These customary frameworks of medication have been in presence for millennia, with a profound information on spices, minerals, and different regular substances. The old Indian texts recorded an abundance of clinical information and restorative definitions.

The advanced drug industry in India started to come to fruition during English pioneer rule. The English acquainted Western medication with India, prompting the foundation of drug organizations for the development of allopathic medications. In the mid twentieth 100 years, the main coordinated drug organizations were established, and they principally centered around delivering and showcasing essential drug definitions.

Post-Freedom Development

Following India's freedom in 1947, the country's drug industry went through tremendous changes. The public authority perceived the significance of the drug area in giving reasonable medical care to the developing populace. The foundation of the Licenses Act in 1970, which permitted just cycle licenses for drugs, assumed a vital part in molding the business.

This approach empowered Indian drug organizations to figure out and create nonexclusive renditions of protected medications, bringing about the accessibility of fundamental medications at reasonable costs. The Indian drug industry's obligation to quality and cost-viability became clear as it provided reasonable prescriptions to not exclusively its homegrown populace yet additionally to numerous different nations confronting wellbeing emergencies.

Worldwide Development and Products

During the 1990s and mid 2000s, India's drug industry saw critical development and worldwide extension. A few Indian drug organizations started to zero in on innovative work, which prompted the revelation of novel medication definitions and the foundation of licensed innovation portfolios. The accentuation on quality and consistence with worldwide administrative guidelines further moved India onto the worldwide drug stage.

Indian drug organizations began extending their impression through trades. The accessibility of superior grade, financially savvy prescriptions made India a center for the development of conventional medications. The presentation of the World Exchange Association's Exchange Related Parts of Licensed innovation Freedoms (Outings) arrangement in 2005 commanded more grounded patent assurance for drugs. This drove Indian organizations to embrace various methodologies, like creating novel medication plans or assembling protected drugs under permit.

The outcome of Indian drug organizations in worldwide business sectors can be ascribed to their vigorous assembling abilities, serious valuing, and adherence to global quality guidelines. This development not just upgraded India's situation in the drug scene yet additionally added to further developing worldwide medical services openness.

Job in Conventional Medication Creation

India's drug industry plays had a basic impact in the development of conventional prescriptions, particularly for life-saving and fundamental medications. The accessibility of minimal expense conventional adaptations of medications has been instrumental in tending to medical services difficulties, especially in emerging nations.

The Indian drug area's emphasis on practical creation techniques and economies of scale has made it conceivable to give fundamental meds for a portion of the expense of their marked partners. This has fundamentally brought down the monetary weight on medical services frameworks and patients, making therapy more available.

As well as assembling conventional adaptations of drugs, Indian drug organizations have been effectively engaged with delivering dynamic drug fixings (APIs), the critical parts of prescriptions. India has laid down a good foundation for itself as a significant provider of APIs to drug organizations around the world, adding to the worldwide accessibility of a large number of drugs.

Innovative work

The advancement of India's drug industry is firmly connected to its obligation to innovative work (Research and development). Throughout the long term, a few Indian drug organizations have put resources into state of the art Research and development offices, finding and creating novel medication definitions, and getting licenses for their advancements.

The attention on Research and development has prompted the rise of Indian drug organizations that have changed from nonexclusive medication producers into research-driven associations. These organizations have fostered a scope of drugs, including biosimilars, which are like biologic medications, and novel treatments for different ailments.

The Indian drug industry's Research and development abilities have brought about huge commitments to worldwide medical services. It has delivered therapies for infections like malignant growth, HIV/Helps, and hepatitis, offering reasonable options in contrast to protected prescriptions. Besides, the improvement of biosimilars has expanded admittance to cutting edge treatments, making them more reasonable for patients around the world.

Challenges Looked by the Drug Business in India

While India's drug industry has encountered surprising development and achievement, it likewise faces a few difficulties and obstructions:

Administrative Consistence: Guaranteeing adherence to global quality and administrative norms can challenge. Indian drug organizations should put vigorously in quality control, producing practices, and consistence with guidelines to keep up with their worldwide standing.

Licensed innovation Freedoms (IPR) Issues: The Outings understanding has achieved a more hearty IPR system, presenting difficulties for the creation of nonexclusive medications. Indian drug organizations need to explore patent regulations and take part in fights in court over the improvement of specific meds.

Quality Affirmation: Keeping up with consistency in item quality and security is significant. Any breaches in quality control can have serious ramifications for patients and can harm an organization's standing.

Fake Medications: The creation and dispersion of fake medications is a worldwide concern. Indian drug organizations should persistently resolve this issue to shield general wellbeing and keep up with the trust of shoppers and administrative bodies.

Value Controls: Government-forced cost controls on fundamental drugs can restrict the benefit of drug organizations. Offsetting reasonable medical services with the supportability of the drug business stays a test.

Rising Research and development Expenses: The expense of innovative work is expanding, especially for novel medication plans. This requires significant ventures and chance taking for drug organizations.

Worldwide Rivalry: As the business turns out to be more aggressive, Indian drug organizations should constantly advance and track down ways of separating themselves in the worldwide market.

Admittance to Medical services: While the business has made significant commitments to further developing medical care openness, there is still work to be finished, especially in remote and underserved areas of India.

The Way Forward

India's drug industry is ready for proceeded with development and effect on worldwide medical services. A few techniques and areas of center can additionally improve the business' commitments:

Interest in Research and development: Proceeded with interest in innovative work, especially in the improvement of imaginative treatments and biosimilars, can additionally reinforce India's situation in the drug scene.

Quality Affirmation: Keeping up with the best expectations of value control and security is basic. Indian drug organizations ought to focus on quality confirmation to support their standing.

Expansion: Investigating assorted remedial regions and venturing into specialty markets can give learning experiences to drug organizations.

Advanced Wellbeing: The reception of computerized wellbeing innovations, telemedicine, and medical services investigation can upgrade patient consideration, making medical care more available and productive.

Worldwide Joint efforts: Coordinated efforts with worldwide drug organizations and research establishments can work with innovation move, information sharing, and progressions in drug improvement.

Natural Obligation: Sticking to manageable and earth dependable practices in drug fabricating is crucial. Organizations ought to consider harmless to the ecosystem fabricating cycles and green drives.

Reasonable Medical services: Endeavors to make fundamental prescriptions more reasonable and available, both in India and on the worldwide stage, ought to proceed. Cooperative drives with legislatures and NGOs can assist with tending to this test.

5.2. Sun Pharmaceutical's Journey

Sun Drug Enterprises, settled in Mumbai, India, has crossed a phenomenal excursion since its beginning. Established in 1983 by Dilip Shanghvi, it began as a somewhat little and nearby drug organization. Nonetheless, throughout the long term, Sun Pharma has developed into one of the world's biggest and most noticeable drug firms. Its way to progress has been set apart by essential acquisitions, a solid obligation to innovative work (Research and development), and an immovable commitment to quality and reasonableness. In this article, we will investigate Sun Drug's surprising excursion, its commitments to the drug business, challenges confronted, and the way ahead in a steadily advancing scene of medical services.

Establishing and Early Development

Sun Drug's process started with a dream to make medical care more open and reasonable. Dilip Shanghvi perceived the requirement for superior grade, yet practical meds in the Indian market. At that point, the drug scene in India was overwhelmed by global organizations, and there was an absence of accentuation on moderateness.

The organization's initial spotlight was on mental medications, taking care of a profoundly particular and underserved fragment of the market. Sun Pharma separated itself through a pledge to quality and development. It put resources into cutting edge producing offices, laying out an establishment for its future development.

One of the significant parts of Sun Pharma's process was its obligation to innovative work. The organization perceived the significance of fostering its own protected innovation and making an arrangement of separated items. This attention on Research and development would recognize Sun Pharma and fuel its journey for greatness.

Key Acquisitions: A Defining moment

In the last part of the 1990s and mid 2000s, Sun Pharma set out on a progression of key acquisitions that would demonstrate instrumental in its development direction. The securing of Caraco Drugs in the US in 1997 checked Sun Pharma's entrance into the worldwide market. This move extended its worldwide impression as well as given admittance to an exceptionally directed and quality-cognizant market.

Notwithstanding, it was the securing of Ranbaxy Research facilities in 2014 that undeniable a turning point in Sun Pharma's set of experiences. At that point, Ranbaxy was perhaps of India's biggest drug organization. The arrangement launch Sun Pharma to the place of the biggest drug organization in India and one of the top nonexclusive medication makers around the world. It likewise carried with it a broad item portfolio, producing capacities, and a significant presence in developing business sectors.

The joining of Ranbaxy into Sun Pharma was a complicated interaction. It included smoothing out tasks, settling administrative issues, and guaranteeing a smooth progress for the two organizations' representatives and partners. Sun Pharma's capacity to effectively explore these difficulties exhibited its administration's sharpness and its obligation to maintaining the greatest norms.

Worldwide Impression and Administrative Consistence

Sun Pharma's extension wasn't restricted to India and the US. The organization has consistently expanded its presence in different worldwide business sectors, including Europe, Japan, and arising economies. These developments were driven by an essential spotlight on administrative consistence, quality confirmation, and the presentation of inventive items.

In the European market, Sun Pharma laid out major areas of strength for a through the obtaining of a few organizations, like Taro Drugs in the US and certain organizations of Novartis in Japan. These moves empowered the organization to get to new business sectors, influence laid out conveyance organizations, and reinforce its item portfolio.

The accentuation on administrative consistence and quality confirmation assumed a vital part in Sun Pharma's worldwide development. The organization's commitment to sticking to the rigid prerequisites of administrative offices in various districts has assisted form with trusting and believability. Sun Pharma put vigorously in powerful quality control measures, cutting edge fabricating offices, and a solid store network to guarantee that its items satisfy the most noteworthy worldwide guidelines.

Innovative work: The Foundation of Development

One of the focal mainstays of Sun Pharma's process has been its steadfast obligation to innovative work. The organization has reliably contributed a huge part of its incomes in Research and development exercises. This commitment to logical examination and advancement has prompted the improvement of a strong item pipeline.

Sun Pharma's Research and development endeavors incorporate a large number of remedial regions, from dermatology and ophthalmology to nervous system science and cardiology. The organization's researchers and scientists work enthusiastically to find and foster new medications, details, and conveyance frameworks. This emphasis on development has brought about areas of strength for a property portfolio, with various licenses and brand names to its name.

Sun Pharma's attention on advancement is obvious in its work in specialty drugs. The organization has created and sent off perplexing and separated items, like inward breath items and biosimilars, which require complex innovation and skill. These undertakings have extended Sun Pharma's portion of the overall industry as well as decidedly affected patient consideration by giving admittance to cutting edge treatment choices.

Worldwide Effect and Commitment to Medical services

Sun Pharma's effect reaches out a long ways past its corporate victories. It assumes a crucial part in tending to worldwide medical care difficulties, especially in the space of reasonableness and admittance to quality drugs. The organization's broad arrangement of conventional medications, biosimilars, and specialty drugs offers financially savvy options in contrast to marked prescriptions, making medical care more available to a huge number of patients around the world.

The presentation of nonexclusive medications by Sun Pharma has been instrumental in lessening medical services costs and expanding admittance to fundamental drugs. Much of the time, the accessibility of these generics has essentially brought down the costs of medications, helping patients and medical services frameworks. The organization's consistent endeavors to create and market top notch generics emphatically affect general wellbeing.

Sun Pharma's introduction to biosimilars, which are bioequivalent adaptations of biologic medications, can possibly change treatment choices for complex sicknesses.

Biosimilars are in many cases more reasonable than their biologic partners, making progressed treatments open to a more extensive populace. Sun Pharma's biosimilar portfolio, covering regions like oncology and immunology, addresses a huge commitment to medical care around the world.

In specialty drugs, Sun Pharma has presented imaginative medicines for conditions like psoriasis, epilepsy, and visual sicknesses. These therapies improve patient consideration as well as deal special restorative choices for complex ailments.

Corporate Obligation and Supportability

Sun Pharma perceives the significance of corporate obligation and supportability. The organization is focused on moral strategic approaches, straightforwardness, and great administration. It sticks to severe quality and security guidelines, guaranteeing the security and prosperity of its representatives and the networks wherein it works.

Supportability is a center part of Sun Pharma's corporate methodology. The organization is aware of its ecological effect and is effectively attempting to lessen its carbon impression. Drives like energy preservation, squander the executives, and mindful water utilization are indispensable to its manageability endeavors. Sun Pharma likewise upholds social and local area government assistance programs that attention on medical services, training, and expertise improvement.

Difficulties and Future Possibilities

While Sun Pharma's process has been portrayed by various accomplishments and achievements, it has not been without its portion of difficulties. The drug business is exceptionally serious and dependent upon rigid administrative oversight. Estimating pressures, expanding contest, and advancing medical services arrangements in various districts present continuous difficulties.

Right after these difficulties, Sun Pharma proceeds to adjust and develop. The organization's versatility and capacity to explore the mind boggling scene of the drug business are demonstrative of its obligation to long haul maintainability and development. Sun Pharma's essential broadening, interest in Research and development, and worldwide extension position it well for what's in store.

What's to come possibilities for Sun Pharma seem promising. The organization's obligation to advancement and the improvement of complicated generics, biosimilars, and specialty drugs are supposed to drive development. The rising commonness of persistent infections and the interest for cutting edge medicines give critical open doors to the organization to have a constructive outcome on medical services.

Sun Pharma's venture into computerized wellbeing and telemedicine is one more sign of its ground breaking approach. The organization's interests in computerized medical services stages and telehealth administrations mirror its obligation to improving patient consideration, openness, and accommodation.

Sun Drug Businesses' excursion from its unassuming starting points to turning into a worldwide drug monster is a demonstration of its pioneer, Dilip Shanghvi, and the committed group that has driven its prosperity. The organization's faithful spotlight on quality, innovative work, and development has made it a foundation of India's drug industry.

Sun Pharma's commitments stretch out past corporate achievement. It assumes a critical part in making medical services more open and reasonable through the presentation of conventional medications and biosimilars. Its obligation to manageability and corporate obligation highlights its devotion to moral strategic policies thus.

5.3. Research and Innovation

Exploration and advancement are crucial drivers of progress and development in different fields, including science, innovation, medical services, and business. They are naturally connected, with research filling in as the establishment whereupon advancement is constructed. In this paper, we will investigate the pivotal job of examination and advancement in propelling society, the exchange between the two, and the different ways they influence various areas of the economy and human existence.

Figuring out Exploration

Research is an orderly course of request and examination pointed toward extending information, taking care of issues, and resolving questions. It is a fundamental apparatus for getting data, testing theories, and creating new experiences. Research takes on different structures, including essential or basic exploration, applied research, and trial research.

Essential Exploration: Essential examination, frequently alluded to as key or unadulterated examination, is interest driven. It tries to grow how we might interpret the normal world and the universe. This kind of exploration might not have prompt commonsense applications but rather lays the preparation for future revelations. Instances of essential examination remember reads up for hypothetical physical science, astronomy, and molecule science.

Applied Exploration: Applied research, then again, is coordinated towards taking care of explicit issues or resolving viable issues. It tries to utilize the information acquired through fundamental exploration to make substantial arrangements. For example, applied research in medication can prompt the improvement of new medications or clinical gadgets.

Trial Exploration: Exploratory examination includes planning controlled investigations to test theories and assemble observational information. It is normally utilized in logical fields to explore circumstances and logical results connections. Clinical preliminaries to evaluate the viability of another medication are an illustration of trial research in medical services.

Research is a dynamic and developing interaction that adjusts to the necessities and difficulties of society. It is led by specialists, researchers, scholastics, and experts across different disciplines. Research is frequently subsidized by states, confidential associations, scholastic establishments, and exploration awards. The results of examination can incorporate new disclosures, logical leap forwards, the improvement of imaginative innovations, and a more profound comprehension of mind boggling peculiarities.

The Job of Development

Development is the method involved with deciphering novel thoughts, information, and disclosures into down to earth applications that make esteem.

It takes many structures, including item development, process advancement, plan of action advancement, and social advancement. Advancement drives progress and financial development, as it prompts the improvement of new items, administrations, and ventures.

Item Advancement: Item development includes the formation of new or further developed labor and products. It can prompt the presentation of earth shattering advances and the improvement of items that upgrade the personal satisfaction. Instances of item advancement incorporate the presentation of cell phones, electric vehicles, and clinical gadgets.

Process Development: Interaction advancement centers around working on the strategies and frameworks used to deliver labor and products. It expects to increment effectiveness, decrease expenses, and improve the nature of result. Process development can prompt progressions in assembling, strategies, and store network the board.

Plan of action Development: Plan of action advancement includes reexamining how an organization makes, conveys, and catches esteem. It can prompt problematic changes in ventures and the making of altogether new plans of action. Organizations like Airbnb and Uber have reformed the neighborliness and transportation areas through plan of action advancement.

Social Development: Social advancement tends to cultural difficulties and looks to make positive social and ecological effects. It can prompt the improvement of inventive answers for issues like neediness, training, medical care, and natural supportability.

Development isn't restricted to the innovation area; it applies to all businesses and fields. It very well may be driven by organizations, research establishments, government offices, and non-benefit associations. The effective execution of development frequently requires cooperation, venture, and an eagerness to face challenges.

The Exchange Among Exploration and Development

Examination and development are firmly interwoven, with each taking care of into the other. Research gives the underpinning of information, revelations, and experiences whereupon development is fabricated. Without research, there would be restricted or no new information to convert into down to earth arrangements. Simultaneously, advancement frequently rouses new examination questions and areas of request.

Research frequently creates groundbreaking thoughts and ideas that can possibly be changed into inventive items, administrations, or cycles. For instance, logical examination in materials science might prompt the advancement of novel materials with remarkable properties that can be utilized in different ventures. These materials can then turn into the reason for creative items and applications.

On the other hand, development can drive the requirement for additional exploration. As new advancements and items are created, questions emerge about their wellbeing, adequacy, and effect on society. This prompts scientists to research and concentrate on these perspectives, prompting a more profound comprehension and refinement of the development.

A perfect representation of the exchange among exploration and development should be visible in the field of medical services. Clinical examination frequently prompts the revelation of new medications and medicines, which are then converted into imaginative medical care arrangements. This interaction includes thorough clinical preliminaries and research to guarantee the security and adequacy of the advancement.

The joint effort between research foundations and industry is one more outline of the collaboration among exploration and advancement. Research directed at colleges and research focuses can be the wellspring of leap forwards that are popularized by organizations and transformed into effective developments. At times, examination and development happen inside a similar association, as is much of the time the case in innovation organizations.

The Effect of Exploration and Development

The effect of exploration and advancement is significant and broad, reaching out to different areas and parts of human existence. The accompanying segments feature a portion of the key regions where exploration and development have had a massive effect.

1. **Medical care and Medication:**
   Exploration and advancement have reformed medical services and medication. The improvement of antibodies, anti-toxins, and high level clinical medicines has broadened human existence hope and diminished death rates. Clinical imaging advancements, for example, X-ray and CT examines, have worked on analytic precision. Developments in telemedicine have upgraded admittance to medical care administrations, particularly in remote and underserved regions.
2. **Innovation and Data:**
   The innovation area is driven by tenacious development. The improvement of the web, cell phones, and man-made brainpower has changed the manner in which individuals convey, access data, and lead business. Research in software engineering and information examination has prompted notable applications in fields, for example, AI and information driven navigation.
3. **Energy and Climate:**
   Exploration and advancement are fundamental for tending to worldwide ecological difficulties. Progresses in environmentally friendly power advancements,

for example, sunlight based and wind power, have diminished dependence on petroleum products and diminished ozone depleting substance outflows. Energy-proficient structures and transportation frameworks add to maintainability. Research in environment science illuminates strategies and activities to alleviate environmental change.

4. **Farming and Food Creation:**
   Developments in horticulture have expanded crop yields and food creation, assisting with taking care of the world's developing populace. Research in biotechnology has prompted hereditarily altered crops that are impervious to irritations and illnesses. Accuracy agribusiness, empowered by innovation and information examination, improves cultivating practices and asset use.
5. **Transportation:**
   Developments in transportation have made travel quicker, more secure, and more helpful. The improvement of electric vehicles (EVs) diminishes fossil fuel byproducts and reliance on petroleum products. Independent vehicles, controlled by computerized reasoning and sensors, can possibly further develop street security and proficiency.
6. **Training:**
   Research in training illuminates showing strategies, educational plan improvement, and instructive approaches. Developments in web-based schooling and e-learning stages have extended admittance to quality training. The utilization of advanced devices and innovations improves the opportunity for growth.
7. **Space Investigation:**

Exploration and advancement have empowered humankind to investigate the universe. The advancement of room innovations and space apparatus has considered missions to different planets, the investigation of heavenly bodies, and the quest for extraterrestrial life. Space investigation encourages logical revelation and moves people in the future.

Challenges in Exploration and Development

While exploration and advancement offer huge advantages to society, they are not without difficulties and intricacies. A portion of the key difficulties include:

Subsidizing: Exploration and advancement require significant speculation. Getting subsidizing can be testing, especially for long haul or high-risk projects.

Moral and Administrative Issues: Advancements in fields, for example, biotechnology and man-made reasoning raise moral and administrative worries. Offsetting progress with moral contemplations is a perplexing errand.

Licensed innovation Freedoms: The assurance of protected innovation is fundamental for empowering development. Be that as it may, finding some kind of harmony among insurance .

Chapter 6

Dr. Reddy's Laboratories - Pioneering Medicine and Research

Dr. Reddy's Labs, an unmistakable drug organization situated in India, has been at the front of spearheading medication and examination for quite some time. Laid out in 1984 by Dr. Kallam Anji Reddy, the organization has developed into a worldwide forerunner in the field of drugs, biotechnology, and examination. Dr. Reddy's Research centers is eminent for its obligation to development, quality, and moderateness in medical services, making it a vital player in the medical services industry.

The excursion of Dr. Reddy's Labs started with a dream to make reasonable and top notch meds open to individuals around the world. Dr. Kallam Anji Reddy, the organizer, was a visionary business person who put stock in the capability of the Indian drug industry to have a massive effect on worldwide medical services. His enthusiasm and devotion established the groundwork for an organization that would proceed to change the drug scene.

One of the key factors that set Dr. Reddy's Labs separated from its rivals is serious areas of strength for its on innovative work. The organization has reliably put resources into state of the art examination, advancement, and innovation. This obligation to Research and development has prompted the improvement of a great many excellent conventional and imaginative drugs, taking special care of different helpful regions.

Dr. Reddy's Labs has a broad worldwide presence, with tasks in excess of 25 nations, including the US, Europe, Russia, and developing business sectors in Asia and Latin America. This worldwide reach permits the organization to serve patients in different districts and add to further developing medical care results on a worldwide scale.

Lately, the drug business has seen a huge shift towards biotechnology and complex generics. Dr. Reddy's Research centers has effectively embraced this change and put resources into biologics and biosimilars, exhibiting its obligation to meeting the advancing requirements of patients and medical services suppliers. The organization's biosimilars portfolio incorporates items that treat conditions like disease, diabetes, and immune system problems, advancing its effect on worldwide medical care.

One of the signs of Dr. Reddy's Labs is its devotion to quality and consistence. The organization sticks to the best guidelines and has gotten various certificates and honors for its assembling offices. This obligation to quality has procured the trust of medical care experts and patients around the world, making Dr. Reddy's a dependable wellspring of drugs.

Dr. Reddy's Labs' obligation to development reaches out past its item portfolio. The organization effectively teams up with scholarly foundations, research associations, and drug organizations to drive forward leaps in drug revelation and advancement. Such organizations empower the organization to get to state of the art advancements and skill, cultivating a culture of development inside the association.

Besides, Dr. Reddy's Labs puts serious areas of strength for an on manageability and corporate social obligation. The organization has attempted different drives to decrease its natural impression and add to the prosperity of the networks it serves. These endeavors line up with the organization's vision of making a better and more feasible world.

As the world wrestles with wellbeing challenges like the Coronavirus pandemic, Dr. Reddy's Research facilities has been at the very front of the reaction, effectively engaged with the turn of events and appropriation of antibodies and medicines. The organization's commitment to propelling medical services arrangements is obvious in its quick reaction to worldwide wellbeing emergencies.

All in all, Dr. Reddy's Labs has arisen as a spearheading force in the field of drugs and examination. Its organizer, Dr. Kallam Anji Reddy, established the groundwork for an organization that has reliably pushed the limits of development, quality, and reasonableness in medical care. With a solid spotlight on innovative work, a worldwide presence, a promise to biotechnology, and a devotion to quality, Dr. Reddy's Research facilities has turned into a confided in name in the drug business. Its endeavors to drive development, embrace manageability, and answer worldwide wellbeing moves highlight its main goal to make a better world for all.

Dr. Reddy's Labs, a main drug organization situated in India, has been a trailblazer in the field of medication and examination since its commencement in 1984. Established by Dr. Kallam Anji Reddy, this organization has developed to turn into a worldwide pioneer, known for its resolute obligation to development, quality, and reasonable medical care arrangements. Throughout the long term, Dr. Reddy's Research facilities plays had a critical impact in molding the drug business and adding to progressions in medication.

At the core of the organization's process lies a dream that rose up out of Dr. Kallam Anji Reddy's confidence in making top notch medications open to individuals around the world. His pioneering soul and devotion gave the driving force to an organization that would proceed to reclassify the drug scene in India and then some.

What sets Dr. Reddy's Labs separated is its steady spotlight on innovative work (Research and development). The organization has reliably put resources into cutting edge examination, development, and innovation. This faithful obligation to Research and development has prompted the improvement of a huge range of top notch nonexclusive and creative prescriptions, tending to different helpful regions.

Dr. Reddy's Labs has laid out a worldwide impression, with tasks in excess of 25 nations, including the US, Europe, Russia, and developing business sectors in Asia and Latin America. This worldwide reach empowers the organization to take special care of patients in different districts, adding to further developed medical services results on a worldwide scale.

Lately, the drug business has seen a huge shift towards biotechnology and complex generics. Dr. Reddy's Research facilities has embraced this change and put resources into biologics and biosimilars, reaffirming its obligation to meeting the advancing requirements of patients and medical care suppliers. The organization's biosimilars portfolio envelops items that treat conditions like disease, diabetes, and immune system problems, further setting its effect on worldwide medical care.

A foundation of Dr. Reddy's Labs is its enduring obligation to quality and consistence. The organization sticks to the best principles and has gotten various certificates and awards for its assembling offices. This devotion to quality has acquired the trust of medical services experts and patients around the world, laying out Dr. Reddy's as a trustworthy wellspring of drugs.

Past its item portfolio, Dr. Reddy's Labs is additionally dedicated to encouraging advancement through joint efforts with scholastic establishments, research associations, and drug organizations. These organizations furnish the organization with admittance to state of the art innovations and mastery, developing a culture of development inside the association.

Moreover, Dr. Reddy's Labs puts areas of strength for an on supportability and corporate social obligation. The organization has sent off different drives pointed toward diminishing its ecological effect and adding to the prosperity of the networks it serves. These endeavors line up with the organization's vision of making a better and more maintainable world.

Notwithstanding worldwide wellbeing difficulties like the Coronavirus pandemic, Dr. Reddy's Research centers has been a proactive member in the reaction, effectively participated in the turn of events and dissemination of immunizations and medicines. The organization's obligation to propelling medical care arrangements is clear in its quick reaction to worldwide wellbeing emergencies.

6.1. Generics and Beyond

The drug business has seen a wonderful development over the course of the last 100 years, and quite possibly of the main headway has been the turn of events and expansion of nonexclusive prescriptions. Generics are, basically, copycat forms of brand-name medicates that offer similar helpful advantages yet for a portion of the expense. They play had a vital impact in making fundamental drugs more open to individuals overall and have turned into a foundation of current medical care frameworks.

The Ascent of Nonexclusive Drugs

The historical backdrop of nonexclusive drugs can be followed back to the mid twentieth hundred years, yet it was only after the mid-twentieth century that they started to acquire noticeable quality. The development of nonexclusive medications can be credited to a few key variables:

Patent Lapse: One of the essential drivers of conventional meds' rise was the termination of licenses on many brand-name drugs. At the point when a medication's patent security closes, it opens the entryway for other drug organizations to create nonexclusive variants of the medicine. This opposition in the market commonly prompts lower costs, making these medications more reasonable for patients.

Cost Reserve funds: The expense viability of conventional medications is a huge benefit. Conventional producers don't have to put resources into the broad innovative work that unique medication organizations do, nor do they have similar showcasing and publicizing costs. These expense reserve funds are given to customers, making generics an appealing choice for those looking for reasonable medical care.

Administrative Structure: Legislatures and administrative organizations all over the planet have set up frameworks to guarantee the security, adequacy, and nature of nonexclusive medications. These administrative cycles give a degree of certainty to patients and medical care suppliers, further supporting the development of the nonexclusive drug industry.

Growing Medical care Access: Generics play had a significant impact in extending admittance to fundamental meds, especially in emerging nations. By offering savvy options in contrast to costly brand-name drugs, they have empowered huge number of individuals to get fundamental therapies for different ailments.

Acknowledgment by Medical services Experts: Over the long haul, medical services experts have become more tolerating of nonexclusive medications, understanding that they offer similar remedial advantages as their image name partners. This acknowledgment has driven the reception of generics in clinical practice.

Difficulties and Discussions

While the ascent of nonexclusive prescriptions decidedly affects medical services, it has not been without difficulties and debates. A portion of the main points of interest and concerns related with generics include:

Quality Confirmation: Guaranteeing the quality and wellbeing of conventional medications is central. While administrative organizations have tough necessities for the endorsement of conventional meds, worries about the consistency and nature of certain items have emerged. Cases of unacceptable or fake conventional medications have brought up issues about the requirement for progressing observing and authorization.

Bioequivalence: Nonexclusive medications should show bioequivalence to their image name partners, implying that they ought to have a similar dynamic fixing, dose, and viability. Notwithstanding, varieties in assembling processes and idle fixings can prompt contrasts in how a few patients answer generics. This fluctuation has been a disputed matter.

Protected innovation and Patent Issues: The section of nonexclusive contenders into the market upon patent lapse has prompted fights in court and questions between drug organizations. These contentions frequently rotate around the translation of patent regulation and the degree to which generics can imitate the first medication without encroaching on protected innovation privileges.

Drug Deficiencies: While nonexclusive medications have expanded admittance to reasonable prescriptions, they are not invulnerable to store network disturbances and deficiencies. Factors like assembling issues, administrative activities, and expanded request can prompt brief deficiencies of fundamental generics, affecting patient consideration.

Public Discernment: A few patients medical care suppliers actually harbor worries about the viability and wellbeing of nonexclusive meds. Confusions about generics, like questions about their quality and viability, can impact decisions in treatment and endorsing rehearses.

Past Generics: The Advancement of Drugs

While generics play had an essential impact in extending admittance to reasonable prescriptions, the drug business keeps on developing. Past generics, a few huge patterns and improvements are reshaping the business' scene:

Biopharmaceuticals and Biosimilars: Biopharmaceuticals, otherwise called biologics, are an unmistakable classification of medications delivered from living cells or life forms. They have reformed the therapy of illnesses like malignant growth, immune system issues, and diabetes. Biosimilars, much the same as generics for conventional medications, are copycat adaptations of biologics. The turn of events and reception of biosimilars address a huge move toward growing admittance to life-saving medicines while bringing down medical care costs.

Customized Medication: Advances in genomics and atomic science have prompted the rise of customized medication, where medicines are custom-made to a person's hereditary cosmetics. This approach takes into account more designated treatments, limiting incidental effects and expanding treatment viability. The approach of customized medication is changing the way that sicknesses are analyzed and treated.

Advanced Wellbeing and Telemedicine: Computerized wellbeing innovations, including telemedicine, wearable gadgets, and wellbeing applications, are rethinking how medical care is conveyed. Patients can now get to clinical meetings and screen their wellbeing from the solace of their homes. These advancements can possibly further develop medical services access, lessen expenses, and improve patient results.

Drug Reusing: Medication reusing, or drug repositioning, is the act of recognizing new remedial purposes for existing prescriptions. This approach can speed up the improvement of medicines for different infections and conditions, as it use the wellbeing and viability information currently accessible for endorsed drugs.

Man-made consciousness and Medication Disclosure: Computerized reasoning (man-made intelligence) is progressively being utilized in drug revelation and advancement. AI calculations can examine huge datasets, recognize potential medication up-and-comers, and anticipate their security and adequacy. This utilization of simulated intelligence can possibly facilitate the medication improvement process and diminish research costs.

Accuracy Medication: Accuracy medication includes fitting medicines to a singular's exceptional hereditary, ecological, and way of life factors. This approach plans to advance treatment, limit aftereffects, and work on understanding results. Accuracy medication is especially encouraging in the areas of oncology and uncommon sicknesses.

Regenerative Medication: Regenerative medication holds the commitment of fixing or supplanting harmed tissues and organs, offering new expectation for patients with conditions that were recently viewed as hopeless. Undifferentiated organism treatment, tissue designing, and quality altering are key parts of this arising field.

The Fate of Medical care

The drug business' development is inseparably connected to the more extensive change of medical care. Propels in drugs, joined with changes in medical care conveyance, patient commitment, and the utilization of information and innovation, are reshaping the eventual fate of medication. Here are a portion of the key viewpoints that will characterize the medical care scene in the years to come:

Patient-Driven Care: The shift towards patient-focused care is reclassifying the medical services insight. Patients are turning out to be more dynamic members in their own wellbeing, with admittance to data and devices that enable them to pursue informed choices. This change puts a more noteworthy accentuation on preventive consideration, early finding, and customized treatment plans.

Esteem Based Medical services: The customary charge for-administration model is giving method for esteeming based medical care, where suppliers are repaid in view of patient results and the nature of care conveyed. This approach plans to work on the proficiency and viability of medical services while diminishing expenses.

Telehealth and Remote Observing: Telemedicine and remote checking advances have acquired noticeable quality, particularly following the Coronavirus pandemic. These developments give helpful admittance to medical care benefits and empower the constant following of patients' wellbeing, especially for those with persistent circumstances.

Huge Information and Examination: The medical services industry is progressively depending on enormous information and investigation to work on persistent consideration, improve clinical independent direction, and upgrade medical services tasks. The examination of enormous datasets can reveal examples and patterns that lead to additional viable medicines and mediations.

Interoperability and Wellbeing Data Trade: Consistent information trade between medical services suppliers, frameworks, and organizations is basic to accomplishing thorough patient consideration. Endeavors to lay out interoperable electronic wellbeing records and wellbeing data trade stages mean to work with this information sharing.

Preventive and Way of life Medication: The attention on preventive and way of life medication is developing, with an accentuation on tending to the main drivers of illnesses through better ways of life, sustenance, and exercise. This approach can prompt better generally wellbeing results and diminished medical care costs.

Worldwide Wellbeing Drives: The world is progressively interconnected with regards to wellbeing. Worldwide wellbeing drives and joint efforts have become fundamental for tending to transnational wellbeing challenges, for example, pandemics, environment related wellbeing gambles, and the spread of irresistible sicknesses.

6.2. Expanding Research and Development

Innovative work (Research and development) are the backbone of progress and development across a large number of businesses, yet they hold an especially focal job in the drug and biotechnology areas. In this article, we will dive into the meaning of Research and development in the domain of medical services, investigating the fundamental elements of innovative work, the significant drivers of Research and development extension, and the effect of this extension on the drug and biotechnology businesses, as well as the more extensive medical services scene.

The Fundamental Elements of Innovative work

Innovative work envelop a bunch of exercises that expect to make new information, advancements, and items. With regards to the drug and biotechnology enterprises, Research and development is a complex interaction with an essential spotlight on the disclosure and improvement of new medications, treatments, and clinical innovations. Here are the vital elements of Research and development in these areas:

Drug Revelation: The most common way of distinguishing new mixtures, particles, or natural specialists that can possibly become drugs. This stage includes broad examination, target distinguishing proof, and the assessment of compound libraries to track down promising possibility for additional turn of events.

Preclinical Exploration: Before another medication can be tried in people, it should go through preclinical examination to assess its security and viability. This stage includes broad research center and creature testing to assemble information on the compound's poisonousness, pharmacokinetics, and pharmacodynamics.

Clinical Preliminaries: Clinical preliminaries are a basic piece of medication advancement, comprising of a progression of stages (Stage I, Stage II, and Stage III) that evaluate the security and viability of the medication in human subjects. These preliminaries include thorough testing, information assortment, and investigation to decide the medication's appropriateness for endorsement.

Administrative Endorsement: When clinical preliminaries are effectively finished, drug organizations submit applications to administrative offices, like the U.S. Food and Medication Organization (FDA) or the European Meds Office (EMA), for endorsement to market and sell the medication.

Post-Market Reconnaissance: After a medication is supported and available, post-market observation guarantees continuous checking of its security and viability in true clinical practice. Any antagonistic occasions or surprising incidental effects are accounted for and surveyed.

Innovation Advancement: Research and development additionally stretches out to the improvement of state of the art advances, apparatuses, and gear utilized in medical services, like analytic gadgets, imaging frameworks, and restorative hardware.

The drug and biotechnology businesses have reliably depended on innovative work to drive advancement and carry new medicines to patients. This has brought about huge progressions in medical care, with various life-saving and life-further developing meds and treatments created through Research and development endeavors.

Significant Drivers of Research and development Extension

The extension of innovative work in the drug and biotechnology ventures is powered by a few key elements:

Expanding Worldwide Illness Weight: The worldwide weight of sickness keeps on ascending, with new difficulties arising, for example, irresistible infection episodes and non-transmittable sicknesses like malignant growth and diabetes. This requires progressing Research and development endeavors to foster medicines and preventive measures.

Mechanical Progressions: Advances in innovation, especially in fields like genomics, proteomics, and information examination, have empowered scientists to more readily grasp illness components, recognize restorative targets, and speed up drug revelation.

Interest for Customized Medication: The shift toward customized medication, where medicines are custom-made to a person's hereditary cosmetics and explicit infection qualities, has provoked an interest for designated treatments. This approach requires broad innovative work to distinguish and foster appropriate medicines.

Developing Maturing Populace: The maturing populace is more helpless to constant sicknesses and age-related conditions, driving the requirement for Research and development in regions like geriatrics, nervous system science, and muscular health.

Developing Business sectors: Drug and biotechnology organizations are progressively extending their tasks into developing business sectors, where the interest for medical services and inventive therapies is developing. This development drives Research and development endeavors custom-made to the particular necessities of these locales.

Administrative and Quality Norms: Advancing administrative principles and the accentuation on quality confirmation and wellbeing in drug advancement require progressing Research and development ventures to meet these necessities.

Rivalry and Market Elements: Extreme contest among drug organizations and the need to remain ahead in the market drive Research and development interests in both brand-name and conventional medications.

Pandemic Reaction: Worldwide pandemics, for example, the Coronavirus pandemic, feature the significance of quick innovative work to foster immunizations and medicines despite arising wellbeing emergencies.

The Effect of Research and development Extension

The extension of innovative work significantly affects the drug and biotechnology ventures, as well as the more extensive medical care scene. Here are a portion of the vital results of Research and development extension:

Advancement and New Medication Improvement: Research and development extension prompts expanded development, bringing about the disclosure and advancement of new medications and treatments that address neglected clinical requirements. These developments can change the treatment and the board of sicknesses, working on tolerant results and personal satisfaction.

Customized Medication: With extended Research and development endeavors, the field of customized medication is progressing quickly. Custom-made medicines in view of hereditary, atomic, and clinical information are turning out to be more available, prompting more successful and exact treatments with less secondary effects.

Expanded Admittance to Medical care: Research and development extension can possibly build admittance to medical services and therapies, particularly in underserved and developing business sectors. By creating financially savvy prescriptions and treatments, drug and biotechnology organizations can make medical care more reasonable and available.

Financial Development: The drug and biotechnology businesses are huge supporters of the economy, making position, creating income, and advancing monetary development. Research and development extension drives further financial improvement by supporting a gifted labor force and encouraging development.

Upper hands: Drug organizations that put vigorously in Research and development gain an upper hand by offering imaginative medications for sale to the public. These organizations can separate themselves in the business and order a more grounded market position.

Logical Joint effort: Research and development extension frequently includes cooperation with scholastic establishments, research associations, and different organizations. These organizations add to the trading of information and skill, encouraging a cooperative examination biological system.

Worldwide Wellbeing Readiness: The capacity to quickly answer arising wellbeing emergencies, like pandemics, is supported by Research and development extension. It empowers the advancement of antibodies and medicines in record time, further developing worldwide wellbeing readiness.

Upgraded Administrative Consistence: Drug organizations should meet severe administrative prerequisites for drug endorsement and wellbeing.

Research and development extension brings about the improvement of powerful administrative practices and consistence techniques, guaranteeing that medications fulfill the most noteworthy guidelines of value and wellbeing.

As of late, the worldwide local area saw the momentous speed at which immunizations and medicines for Coronavirus were created and sent, exhibiting the effect of Research and development extension on worldwide wellbeing. The drug and biotechnology enterprises, upheld by vigorous innovative work endeavors, assumed a significant part in answering the pandemic.

Difficulties and Contemplations

While the extension of innovative work holds huge potential for propelling medical care, it isn't without its difficulties and contemplations:

High Improvement Expenses: Growing new medications and treatments is an exorbitant and tedious interaction. High improvement expenses can restrict the reasonableness and availability of new medicines, especially in asset compelled locales.

Moral and Administrative Issues: Moral contemplations encompassing the direct of clinical preliminaries and examination, as well as developing administrative norms, require close regard for guarantee that Research and development endeavors are led mindfully and morally.

Information Protection and Security: The assortment and examination of immense measures of wellbeing related information in Research and development raise worries about information protection and security. Safeguarding patient data and agreeing with information security guidelines are fundamental contemplations.

Wellbeing Disparities: Research and development extension ought to address wellbeing imbalances by guaranteeing that new medicines and treatments are available to all, paying little heed to financial status or geographic area.

Protected innovation: Safeguarding licensed innovation privileges is significant for cultivating development and empowering Research and development ventures. Finding some kind of harmony among security and data sharing is a key thought.

Economical Practices: Research and development extension ought to integrate manageable and naturally dependable practices to limit the ecological effect of medication advancement and assembling.

Worldwide Cooperation: Cooperative endeavors across boundaries and districts are fundamental to tending to worldwide wellbeing challenges. Global associations can upgrade the adequacy of Research and development in handling sicknesses and wellbeing emergencies.

6.3. Global Pharmaceutical Impact

The drug business assumes a crucial part in worldwide wellbeing and the prosperity of billions of individuals. It is a complex area incorporating research, improvement, assembling, and conveyance of drugs that save lives, ease enduring, and upgrade the personal satisfaction. The effect of the drug business stretches out a long ways past the bounds of science and business, impacting medical services frameworks, economies, and general wellbeing strategies around the world. In this exhaustive conversation, we will dig into the assorted aspects of the worldwide drug influence, investigating its commitment to general wellbeing, monetary development, admittance to prescriptions, and difficulties and discussions it faces.

Drug Industry and General Wellbeing

The most central effect of the drug business is on general wellbeing. Prescriptions are fundamental devices in the counteraction, conclusion, and therapy of many sicknesses and ailments. The drug business' commitments to general wellbeing can be analyzed in a few key regions:

Sickness Counteraction: Immunizations are one of the main commitments of the drug business to general wellbeing. Immunization programs have prompted the annihilation of smallpox, the close end of polio, and the control of numerous other irresistible illnesses. These preventive estimates save a huge number of lives consistently.

Therapy of Ongoing and Intense Circumstances: Drugs give viable therapies to different constant and intense ailments. From anti-toxins that battle bacterial contaminations to antiretroviral drugs that oversee HIV/Helps, prescriptions are basic in controlling, making due, and in any event, restoring illnesses.

The executives of Constant Illnesses: Persistent sicknesses, like diabetes, hypertension, and cardiovascular infections, are common around the world. The drug business creates and supplies meds that empower people to deal with these circumstances actually, working on their personal satisfaction and decreasing the gamble of entanglements.

Progresses in Disease Treatment: The improvement of designated treatments and immunotherapies has changed malignant growth treatment. These forward leaps have further developed the endurance rates and personal satisfaction for disease patients, introducing another period in oncology.

Psychological wellness: Drugs for emotional well-being conditions, including gloom, uneasiness, and schizophrenia, have changed the treatment scene. They assist people with driving additional satisfying lives and add to destigmatizing psychological wellness issues.

Interesting Infections: Drugs for uncommon illnesses, frequently alluded to as vagrant medications, have furnished trust for patients with conditions that were recently ignored because of their restricted predominance. The drug business has taken critical steps in creating medicines for uncommon and vagrant illnesses.

Torment The board: The drug business creates a scope of prescriptions for torment the executives, working on the solace and prosperity of people with intense or constant torment conditions.

Maternal and Youngster Wellbeing: Drugs play had a critical impact in maternal and kid wellbeing, guaranteeing safe pregnancies, labor, and neonatal consideration. Prescriptions for pre-birth nutrients, work acceptance, and neonatal consideration add to solid pregnancies and labor.

Crisis Medication: In crises, like mishaps, catastrophic events, and pandemics, drugs are fundamental. They give medicines to wounds, contaminations, and intense circumstances during emergencies.

The drug business' commitments to general wellbeing are certain, with headways in drug revelation and advancement essentially expanding future and personal satisfaction. Notwithstanding, challenges exist, like admittance to drugs, reasonableness, and the weight of non-transferable sicknesses (NCDs), which keep on being a worldwide general wellbeing concern.

Financial Effect of the Drug Business

Notwithstanding its job in general wellbeing, the drug business is a significant driver of financial development. It is a huge supporter of public economies, giving business, producing income, and supporting innovative work. The financial effect of the drug business is obvious in different viewpoints:

Business: The drug business is a work concentrated area, utilizing a great many individuals internationally. This incorporates analysts, researchers, drug specialists, fabricating staff, deals and advertising experts, administrative specialists, and authoritative faculty. Notwithstanding immediate business, the business makes occupations in related fields, like strategies, appropriation, and medical services.

Innovative work Speculation: The drug business puts vigorously in innovative work. These speculations drive development, spike financial development, and make an expanding influence across related businesses, including biotechnology, medical services, and the scholarly world.

Licensed innovation and Advancement: Licensed innovation privileges, like licenses, are significant in the drug business. They boost advancement by giving transitory restraining infrastructures to organizations that foster new medications. These licenses energize interest in Research and development and the advancement of novel treatments.

Income and Benefit: Drug organizations produce significant income and benefit, adding to financial development. The offer of prescriptions and clinical items is a significant type of revenue for these organizations.

Commodity and Exchange: Drug items are huge supporters of global exchange. Numerous nations send out drugs to worldwide business sectors, assisting with adjusting import/export imbalances and animate financial development.

Store network and Coordinated factors: The drug business is intently attached to inventory network and strategies activities, setting out open doors in transportation, warehousing, and dissemination. Guaranteeing the effective conveyance of prescriptions is urgent to worldwide medical care.

Monetary Bunches: The drug business frequently frames financial groups, with research offices, fabricating plants, and drug center points packed in unambiguous locales. These bunches set out open doors for business advancement, scholarly coordinated effort, and financial turn of events.

Medical services Spending: While medical care spending is a different classification, it is firmly connected to the drug business' financial effect. The interest for prescriptions and medical care administrations drives medical care uses, which, thus, add to financial development.

Biotechnology Progressions: The convergence of biotechnology and drugs has prompted headways in the two areas. Biotechnology firms and drug organizations frequently work together, cultivating development and monetary development.

Generics and Reasonable Meds: The turn of events and assembling of conventional medications have made fundamental drugs more reasonable and available, helping medical care frameworks and economies.

The financial effect of the drug business reaches out to both created and agricultural nations. In the last option, the business adds to financial development, work creation, and admittance to fundamental meds, supporting endeavors to accomplish the Manageable Advancement Objectives (SDGs).

Admittance to Medications and Worldwide Wellbeing Value

While the drug business' commitments to general wellbeing and the economy are impressive, admittance to medications stays a worldwide test. Abberations in admittance to fundamental drugs persevere, with different elements affecting worldwide wellbeing value:

Moderateness: The expense of drugs can be a boundary to get to, particularly for people without health care coverage or those living in low-and center pay nations. High medication costs can restrict admittance to life-saving medicines.

Protected innovation Freedoms: Licenses and protected innovation privileges can confine the accessibility of reasonable nonexclusive renditions of prescriptions, especially for new and expensive medications. Admittance to drugs can be postponed because of patent eliteness.

Administrative Obstructions: Administrative prerequisites and endorsement cycles can influence the accessibility of prescriptions in various areas. Postpones in administrative endorsements can restrict admittance to therapies, particularly for patients with earnest clinical requirements.

Store network Difficulties: Issues connected with the store network, for example, stockouts, transportation obstructions, and circulation challenges, can thwart admittance to prescriptions, especially in remote or underserved regions.

Wellbeing Framework: Lacking medical care foundation, including medical clinics, facilities, and prepared medical services experts, can restrict admittance to conclusion and therapy. The accessibility of prescriptions is intently attached to the limit of medical care frameworks.

Dismissed Illnesses: A few infections, frequently alluded to as disregarded tropical sicknesses (NTDs), get restricted consideration and examination financing. This can bring about an absence of accessible medicines for these circumstances, influencing populaces in low-asset settings.

Chapter 7

Innovations and Sustainability in Indian Manufacturing

In the domain of Indian assembling, developments and maintainability have become crucial variables that shape the business' direction. The assembling area in India has gone through critical changes throughout the long term, and as we move further into the 21st hundred years, the combination of development and manageability is ready to assume a pivotal part in molding its future.

One of the crucial parts of this change lies in the reception of trend setting innovations, like Industry 4.0, Man-made brainpower (simulated intelligence), the Web of Things (IoT), and robotization. These advances have reformed assembling processes, making them more proficient, financially savvy, and eco-accommodating. In India, the joining of these advancements is steadily turning into a standard as opposed to a special case, encouraging another period of shrewd assembling.

One of the region where these innovations have had a critical effect is in the robotization of creation lines. Indian makers have progressively embraced mechanical computerization, which has further developed accuracy and efficiency as well as added to maintainability by lessening waste and energy utilization. The robotization of dreary and work escalated undertakings has likewise prompted a more secure work space, limiting the gamble of mishaps and wounds. As India keeps on progressing in the robotization area, it is headed to turning into a worldwide center point for imaginative and supportable assembling.

Moreover, artificial intelligence and information examination are assuming a significant part in upgrading fabricating processes. Man-made intelligence calculations are utilized for prescient support, quality control, and request guaging, guaranteeing that assets are utilized proficiently and creation is lined up with market needs. By diminishing machine free time and waste, man-made intelligence contributes altogether to supportability by bringing down the ecological impression of assembling activities.

The reception of IoT gadgets is one more significant advancement in Indian assembling. These interconnected gadgets give continuous information on hardware execution and ecological circumstances, permitting producers to settle on informed choices. For example, sensors in a plant can screen temperature, dampness, and energy utilization, empowering makers to improve energy use, decrease squander, and make a more manageable creation process.

While innovation assumes a vital part in development, featuring the significance of maintainable practices inside the assembling sector is fundamental. Supportability in Indian assembling envelops different aspects, including asset the executives, natural effect, social obligation, and monetary development.

Effective asset the executives is a foundation of manageability. Producers in India are progressively embracing green practices, like reusing and reusing materials, lessening water and energy utilization, and limiting waste age. Thusly, they add to natural preservation as well as save costs over the long haul.

Decreasing the ecological effect is one more basic part of supportability. Indian assembling organizations are changing towards cleaner and greener advances to relieve their carbon impression. This incorporates the utilization of sustainable power sources like sunlight based and wind power, as well as the reception of eco-accommodating creation processes. Accordingly, the assembling area is turning out to be more eco-cognizant, lining up with worldwide endeavors to battle environmental change.

Social obligation is necessary to maintainability, as it includes guaranteeing the prosperity of the labor force and the networks in which fabricating offices are found. Indian makers are progressively putting resources into representative government assistance, wellbeing, and security measures. By giving fair wages, safe working circumstances, and admittance to instruction and medical care, they add to the general prosperity of their representatives and the general public at large.

Financial development with regards to supportability includes encouraging advancement and business venture. Indian assembling is turning into a favorable place for new businesses and little endeavors that emphasis on manageable items and cycles. This prompts monetary development as well as advances development in manageability rehearses. Besides, maintainability drives frequently open up new business sectors and business potential open doors, further powering financial development in the assembling area.

A huge change in outlook can be seen in the manner in which Indian assembling organizations see supportability. It is not generally seen as a simple administrative prerequisite however as an upper hand. Organizations are understanding that embracing manageable practices can prompt expense investment funds, upgraded brand picture, and a more grounded market position. Besides, purchasers are turning out to be all the more earth cognizant, and they favor items from organizations that show a promise to supportability.

One of the critical drivers of manageability in Indian assembling is government strategy and guideline. The Indian government has presented a few drives and strategies pointed toward advancing manageable assembling rehearses. These strategies incorporate monetary motivations for sustainable power reception, stricter natural guidelines, and backing for innovative work in green advancements. Government bodies like the Department of Energy Effectiveness (Honey bee) and the Service of New and Environmentally friendly power (MNRE) play played huge parts in molding the supportability scene of Indian assembling.

Notwithstanding government support, industry affiliations and non-administrative associations (NGOs) have been effectively engaged with advancing maintainability. These associations give direction, lead exploration, and deal certificate programs that urge makers to embrace feasible practices. For example, the Confederation of Indian Industry (CII) has sent off the "GreenCo" rating framework, which evaluates the natural exhibition of organizations and perceives those that succeed in maintainability.

While development and manageability are naturally connected, challenges persevere on the way towards a more practical Indian assembling area. One critical test is the underlying venture expected to carry out green innovations and practices. While these ventures frequently bring about long haul cost investment funds, they can be a boundary for more modest producers with restricted monetary assets.

Another test is the requirement for gifted work. The coordination of cutting edge innovations like man-made intelligence, IoT, and computerization requires a labor force with the important abilities. India is gaining ground in resolving this issue by advancing expertise improvement programs and professional preparation, however it stays a work underway.

Inventory network maintainability is likewise a worry. To accomplish genuine maintainability, producers need to guarantee that their whole store network sticks to comparable natural and moral guidelines. This can be testing, particularly for organizations that source natural substances from locales with remiss guidelines and practices.

Moreover, the checking and revealing of manageability measurements need improvement. While numerous Indian producers have embraced reasonable practices, there is space for improvement in following and revealing key execution pointers. Normalized detailing structures and straightforwardness are critical for surveying progress and benchmarking against industry peers.

The worldwide commercial center assumes a significant part in impacting Indian assembling's way to deal with supportability. As India looks to grow its presence in global business sectors, it should stick to the maintainability assumptions for its exchanging accomplices. Organizations that trade their items to districts with rigid maintainability guidelines are constrained to adjust their practices to these norms. Thus, the globalization of supply chains requires a more complete and predictable way to deal with maintainability in Indian assembling.

Advancement and maintainability are entwined with regards to round economy ideas. A round economy means to limit squander and boost the utilization of assets by stressing item life span, reusing, and reusing materials. Indian makers are bit by bit embracing this methodology by planning items for solidness and recyclability, as well as investigating approaches to reuse squander materials. By embracing round economy standards, they add to natural supportability and encourage inventive answers for asset the executives.

One more aspect of maintainability inside Indian assembling is the development of eco-accommodating and green items. These items are planned in view of negligible ecological effect, utilizing practical materials and cycles. The creation of eco-accommodating items has built up forward momentum in homegrown business sectors as well as opened ways to worldwide clients who esteem manageability. This extension of item contributions cultivates development and expansion inside the assembling area.

Maintainability goes past the plant floor and creation processes; it stretches out to bundling and coordinated factors. Bundling assumes a critical part in decreasing the natural impression of made items. Eco-accommodating bundling materials, as well as creative plans that limit squander and enhance delivering space, are turning out to be more common. Manageable strategies rehearses, for example, proficient course arranging and the utilization of electric or cross breed vehicles, further add to diminishing the carbon impression of the assembling area.

The development of the Indian assembling area is obvious in different businesses, including car, hardware, materials, and environmentally friendly power. The auto business, for instance, is seeing a flood in the creation of electric vehicles (EVs). This progress is driven by the worldwide shift towards supportable transport.

7.1. Technological Advancements

Innovative headways have reliably determined human advancement since the beginning of time. The development of innovation has profoundly impacted social orders, economies, and individual lives, and in the 21st 100 years, the speed of progress has arrived at extraordinary levels. This exposition investigates the extensive effect of mechanical headways in different areas, including correspondence, medical care, transportation, and schooling.

Correspondence Upset

The correspondence scene has been one of the most significantly impacted areas of innovative progressions. The coming of the web and the multiplication of cell phones have upset how individuals interface and offer data. These improvements significantly affect individual connections, business, and the scattering of data.

The web, a worldwide organization of interconnected PCs, has changed the manner in which we access and offer data. It has democratized admittance to information, making it more straightforward for individuals to learn, impart, and team up. Data that was once scant and constrained by a limited handful is presently promptly accessible to anybody with a web association. This has engaged people and associations, empowering them to get to huge measures of information and information to go with informed choices.

Besides, the ascent of online entertainment stages, like Facebook, Twitter, and Instagram, has changed how we interface with each other and consume news. These stages have made new types of correspondence and social communication, permitting individuals to interface with loved ones, share their contemplations and encounters, and draw in with a worldwide crowd. Nonetheless, they have likewise raised worries about security, falsehood, and the effect of protected, closed off areas on open talk.

Cell phones play had a urgent impact in making the web open to an enormous piece of the worldwide populace. These pocket-sized gadgets consolidate correspondence, calculation, and amusement, empowering individuals to convey the force of the web with them any place they go. This has changed how we impart as well as how we work, shop, and engage ourselves. Versatile applications have become fundamental to current life, with administrations going from ride-sharing to food conveyance to wellness following accessible readily available.

Because of these innovative progressions, the world has become more interconnected than any other time in recent memory. Data can be shared right away across the globe, permitting people and associations to team up, advance, and answer worldwide difficulties all the more actually. Nonetheless, the fast scattering of data has additionally presented difficulties, including the spread of falsehood and digital dangers.

Medical services Change

Innovative headways significantly affect the field of medical care. From diagnostics to treatment, innovation has reformed how medical services is conveyed, making it more effective, open, and customized.

One remarkable improvement is the utilization of electronic wellbeing records (EHRs) and telemedicine. EHRs have digitized patient records, making them effectively open to medical services suppliers. This works on the coordination of care as well as lessens clinical mistakes and regulatory expenses. Telemedicine, then again, permits patients to talk with medical care experts from a distance, giving admittance to clinical mastery in underserved regions and empowering more helpful medical services conveyance.

Clinical imaging innovation has likewise seen huge progressions, with the improvement of high-goal imaging methods, for example, attractive reverberation imaging (X-ray) and figured tomography (CT) examines. These advances give more itemized and exact pictures of the human body, supporting the conclusion and therapy of different ailments. Also, 3D printing has been utilized to make patient-explicit inserts and prosthetics, working on the personal satisfaction for some people.

Computerized reasoning (simulated intelligence) and AI are transforming medical care, especially in clinical conclusion and therapy proposals. These advancements can examine huge measures of patient information, helping medical care experts in distinguishing examples and making more exact determinations. Man-made intelligence driven prescient investigation can assist with expecting infection flare-ups, improve emergency clinic activities, and even find new medication up-and-comers.

Customized medication, empowered by headways in genomics and biotechnology, is altering medical care. DNA sequencing and genomic profiling permit medical services suppliers to fit therapies to a person's hereditary cosmetics. This commitments more successful treatments with less incidental effects. In any case, moral worries, including protection and hereditary separation, have emerged as genomic information turns out to be all the more generally available.

Mechanical technology and mechanization have additionally tracked down their place in medical services. Robots are utilized in medical procedures, patient consideration, and recovery. They can perform exact and dull undertakings, lessening the gamble of human mistake and permitting medical services experts to zero in on additional complicated parts of care.

The Coronavirus pandemic highlighted the significance of innovation in medical services. From immunization improvement and dissemination to remote observing of patients, innovation assumed a significant part in answering the emergency. The pandemic sped up the reception of telehealth, further showing its true capacity in conveying medical care administrations.

Transportation Unrest

The manner in which individuals and products move starting with one spot then onto the next has seen a transportation unrest driven by mechanical headways. Developments in transportation have further developed productivity, security, and supportability.

Quite possibly of the main change in transportation is the rise of electric vehicles (EVs). Electric vehicles, controlled by batteries and environmentally friendly power sources, can possibly diminish ozone harming substance discharges and decline the reliance on petroleum derivatives. Legislatures and automakers are putting resources into EV foundation and assembling, making electric transportation a reasonable option in contrast to conventional fuel controlled vehicles.

Besides, independent vehicles, or self-driving vehicles, can possibly reshape the transportation scene. With headways in computer based intelligence and sensor innovation, independent vehicles are turning out to be more equipped for exploring streets securely. These vehicles can possibly lessen mishaps, ease gridlock, and increment versatility for people who can't drive.

Ride-sharing and vehicle sharing stages have acquired prominence, impacting the manner in which individuals contemplate vehicle possession. Administrations like Uber and Lyft give advantageous transportation choices without the requirement for individual vehicles. Vehicle sharing projects, like Zipcar, offer adaptability and cost reserve funds for metropolitan inhabitants.

The avionic business has likewise seen innovative headways, with the improvement of additional eco-friendly and harmless to the ecosystem airplane. The utilization of composite materials, streamlined plan upgrades, and more effective motors add to diminished fuel utilization and lower discharges.

Rapid rail and hyperloop advances are being investigated to further develop land-based transportation. These frameworks can possibly give quick, energy-productive, and feasible methods of movement between urban areas.

In metropolitan regions, miniature portability arrangements, like electric bikes and bicycles, have become famous for brief distance travel. These options assist with lessening clog and discharges in jam-packed urban communities.

The transportation insurgency can possibly lessen the natural effect of movement and make transportation more open and proficient. Nonetheless, challenges remain, including the requirement for thorough foundation enhancements, administrative contemplations for independent vehicles, and tending to the natural effect of electric vehicle creation and charging.

Schooling Change

The field of schooling has been altogether changed by mechanical headways. The joining of innovation in schooling has extended admittance to learning, customized guidance, and the advancement of new educational methodologies.

Online instruction, or e-learning, has made training open to a worldwide crowd. This shift was advanced during the Coronavirus pandemic, with numerous instructive foundations progressing to online stages. Online courses and degree programs permit people to learn at their own speed, making schooling more adaptable and helpful. Be that as it may, admittance to dependable web and computerized gadgets stays a boundary for certain students.

The utilization of instructive innovation, or edtech, has set out new open doors for customized learning. Versatile learning stages use artificial intelligence to modify the opportunity for growth in light of a singular's assets and shortcomings. This approach can assist students with advancing all the more proficiently and successfully.

Open instructive assets (OER) have extended admittance to instructive materials, making reading material and course satisfied uninhibitedly accessible to understudies and instructors. This lessens the monetary weight of instruction and advances more extensive spread of information.

7.2. Commitment to Sustainability

Obligation to manageability is presently not a choice yet a need in the 21st hundred years. The fast development of worldwide populace, expanding industrialization, and asset utilization have put monstrous strain in the world's biological systems. To neutralize these unfavorable effects, legislatures, organizations, and people should put forth a deliberate attempt to embrace feasible practices and decrease their ecological impression. This article dives into the diverse parts of supportability, investigating its importance, the job of different partners, and the difficulties and potential open doors it presents.

The Meaning of Manageability

Manageability includes a wide range of standards and practices pointed toward protecting the planet's biological systems and assets for current and people in the future. It is established in addressing our necessities without compromising the capacity of people in the future to address their own issues. The idea acquired unmistakable quality in the twentieth hundred years with the acknowledgment that unrestrained industrialization and asset exhaustion were not feasible in the long haul.

At its center, supportability comprises of three interconnected points of support: natural, social, and financial. The ecological point of support centers around lessening adverse consequences on the regular world, including decreasing contamination, saving assets, and alleviating environmental change. The social support point frets about impartial admittance to assets, civil rights, and further developing the prosperity of networks. The monetary support point accentuates the requirement for financial development that doesn't come to the detriment of the climate or society. These three support points structure the groundwork of the maintainability idea, frequently alluded to as the "triple primary concern."

The meaning of maintainability is highlighted by a progression of worldwide difficulties. Environmental change, driven by ozone depleting substance outflows, represents an extreme danger to the planet's biological systems and human social orders. Biodiversity misfortune, deforestation, and the corruption of normal territories further fuel the ecological emergency. In addition, issues like neediness, disparity, and admittance to clean water and disinfection keep on influencing billions of individuals all over the planet.

Manageability is essential for moderating these difficulties. By progressing to additional reasonable practices and frameworks, we can diminish the ecological impression, mitigate social abberations, and cultivate monetary versatility. Economical improvement perceives the relationship of these three support points and tries to make an agreeable equilibrium that benefits both current and people in the future.

The Job of Government in Manageability

States assume an essential part in propelling manageability. Through arrangement advancement, guideline, and the portion of assets, states can impact and guide manageable practices in numerous areas. A portion of the key jobs that states play in supportability include:

Strategy Improvement: Legislatures come up with arrangements and methodologies that set the course for supportable turn of events. These arrangements might include environmentally friendly power targets, outflow decrease objectives, land-use arranging, and protection measures. For example, the Paris Arrangement, a worldwide environment accord, shows the way that states can cooperate to address worldwide maintainability challenges.

Guideline: Unofficial laws are significant in deeply shaping way of behaving and empowering supportable practices. These guidelines might include ecological principles, discharges limits, squander the executives rules, and item marking. Administrative structures advance consistence with maintainability standards and make a level battleground for organizations.

Monetary Help: Legislatures frequently give monetary motivations to advance supportability drives. These impetuses may incorporate awards, endowments, tax breaks, and low-interest advances for environmentally friendly power projects, energy-effective structures, or manageable farming. Such monetary help can assist with animating interest in feasible advancements and practices.

Public Framework: States put resources into public foundation that upholds manageability. This incorporates public transportation frameworks, sustainable power lattice foundation, and waste administration offices. These speculations decrease the ecological effect as well as work on the personal satisfaction for residents.

Worldwide Participation: States team up on global drives to address worldwide maintainability challenges. The Unified Countries Manageable Improvement Objectives (SDGs) are a great representation of such participation. These objectives envelop a wide scope of supportability goals, from neediness decrease to clean energy access, and urge countries to cooperate to accomplish them.

Instruction and Mindfulness: Legislatures have the ability to teach and bring issues to light about manageability issues. School educational plans can consolidate ecological and maintainability training, and state run administrations can run public mindfulness missions to advise residents about the significance regarding feasible living.

Innovative work: State run administrations store innovative work drives that help manageability advancement. This remembers ventures for clean energy advances, economical farming practices, and ecological protection research.

The job of government in supportability is mind boggling and multi-layered. While states can establish a favorable climate for manageability, they likewise face difficulties like political tensions, spending plan requirements, and the need to offset monetary development with ecological and social worries.

Organizations and Maintainability

Organizations are central members in the manageability scene. They significantly affect the climate, society, and the worldwide economy, earnestly committing to manageability fundamental. Here are a few manners by which organizations can add to manageability:

Corporate Social Obligation (CSR): Numerous organizations have taken on CSR drives that underline moral and maintainable strategic policies. CSR exercises frequently incorporate local area commitment, natural stewardship, and magnanimous endeavors to address social and ecological difficulties.

Maintainable Production network: Organizations can advance supportability by guaranteeing their inventory fastens stick to moral and natural principles. This might include obtaining maintainable materials, lessening waste, and limiting the carbon impression of creation and dispersion.

Eco-accommodating Items and Administrations: Organizations can create and showcase items and administrations that have a lower natural effect. This might include energy-productive apparatuses, eco-accommodating bundling, or reasonable design lines.

Environmentally friendly power Energy: Organizations can progress to environmentally friendly power sources and embrace energy-productive practices in their tasks. A few enterprises have focused on 100 percent sustainable power, lessening their carbon impression and supporting the change to a perfect energy economy.

Roundabout Economy: The idea of a round economy includes lessening waste and expanding asset productivity. Organizations can assume a crucial part in this by planning items for solidness, repairability, and recyclability.

Maintainability Revealing: Numerous organizations currently distribute manageability reports that detail their ecological and social presentation. These reports give straightforwardness and responsibility to partners and financial backers.

Development: Organizations can drive manageability through exploration and advancement. For instance, progressions in environmentally friendly power, electric vehicles, and reasonable horticulture are many times led by the confidential area.

Representative Commitment: Connecting with workers in maintainability endeavors can improve an organization's obligation to manageability. Empowering representatives to take on reasonable practices in their day to day work and individual lives can make a culture of manageability inside the association.

Manageability isn't just a moral decision for organizations yet additionally an essential one. It can prompt expense investment funds, improve brand notoriety, draw in naturally cognizant shoppers, and lessen long haul chances related with ecological and social issues.

Difficulties and Open doors in Supportability

While the obligation to maintainability is imperative, it accompanies its arrangement of difficulties and potential open doors. Understanding these can help people, associations, and states explore the way towards a more economical future.

Challenges:

Transient versus Long haul Contemplations: One test in maintainability is the strain between momentary monetary interests and long haul natural and social prosperity. Quick monetary worries frequently outweigh longer-term supportability goals.

Intricacy and Interconnectedness: Manageability issues are many times perplexing and interconnected. Resolving one issue can prompt unseen side-effects in another space. For instance, endeavors to decrease water utilization in agribusiness may accidentally prompt expanded energy utilization.

Asset Shortage: As the worldwide populace develops, rivalry for limited assets, like freshwater and arable land, escalates. This asset shortage can prompt contentions and ecological corruption.

Protection from Change: Protection from change, whether in private propensities or strategic policies, can be a critical obstruction to maintainability. Individuals and associations might oppose embracing more maintainable choices because of latency, cost concerns, or an absence of mindfulness.

Ecological Corruption: The debasement of normal biological systems, including deforestation, contamination, and living space misfortune, keeps on undermining biodiversity and environments. Switching this corruption is an impressive test.

Financial Inconsistencies: Monetary incongruities can obstruct manageability endeavors. Non-industrial nations might focus on monetary development over ecological worries, while created nations may consume.

7.3. Global Competitiveness

Worldwide seriousness is a complex idea that impacts the monetary prosperity and outcome of countries in an interconnected world. It envelops an expansive scope of elements, including monetary execution, development, framework, schooling, administration, and the sky is the limit from there. This article investigates the significance of worldwide seriousness, the key determinants, and the procedures that nations can take on to improve their intensity on the world stage.

The Meaning of Worldwide Seriousness

Worldwide seriousness is an essential driver of monetary development and improvement, forming the capacity of countries to flourish in a profoundly cutthroat and interconnected worldwide economy. Intensity stretches out past financial execution; it includes a country's ability to produce and keep up with high expectations for everyday comforts, feasible turn of events, and a decent personal satisfaction for its residents. A few variables add to the meaning of worldwide seriousness:

Financial Development: A country's monetary development is firmly connected to its seriousness. Serious countries are better prepared to draw in ventures, make occupations, and cultivate development, all of which add to supported financial development.

Way of life: Elevated degrees of seriousness by and large convert into a better quality of living for the populace. This incorporates better admittance to training, medical services, and in general prosperity.

Advancement and Business: Seriousness encourages advancement and business venture, driving the improvement of new items, administrations, and innovations. It energizes a culture of consistent improvement and versatility.

Worldwide Exchange: Serious nations have a more grounded presence in global exchange. They are bound to trade labor and products, growing their market reach and creating unfamiliar trade income.

Speculation Fascination: A cutthroat climate is helpful for drawing in both homegrown and unfamiliar ventures. Financial backers are bound to place their cash into nations that offer strength, a gifted labor force, and a business-accommodating climate.

Work Creation: A cutthroat economy commonly produces business open doors. At the point when organizations flourish and grow, they require more laborers, lessening joblessness rates.

Destitution Decrease: Further developed seriousness frequently prompts a diminishing in neediness rates. A flourishing economy can give occupations, raise compensation, and set out open doors for up versatility.

Comprehensive Development: Cutthroat countries hold back nothing, guaranteeing that monetary advantages are circulated all the more impartially across the populace. This lessens pay imbalance and social abberations.

Key Determinants of Worldwide Intensity

Worldwide intensity is impacted by a wide exhibit of determinants that can fluctuate from one country to another. While certain variables are characteristic for a country, others can be impacted through compelling strategies and techniques. Here are a portion of the critical determinants of worldwide seriousness:

Monetary Strength: Financial dependability is a crucial determinant of intensity. Low expansion, stable cash, and a very much directed monetary framework are fundamental for drawing in ventures and encouraging financial development.

Foundation: Quality framework, including transportation, energy, and computerized networks, is vital for financial intensity. Proficient foundation lessens the expense of carrying on with work and upgrades efficiency.

Advancement and Exploration: A solid spotlight on advancement, examination, and improvement is a critical driver of intensity. Putting resources into innovation and cultivating a culture of development can prompt the improvement of new items and cycles.

Training and Labor force: An informed and talented labor force is fundamental for intensity. Countries with a solid accentuation on training and labor force improvement will generally be more versatile and equipped for satisfying the requests of a quickly changing worldwide economy.

Market Size and Access: Admittance to huge and various business sectors, both locally and globally, can improve intensity. It permits organizations to scale their tasks, arrive at a more extensive client base, and exploit economies of scale.

Administrative Climate: A straightforward, effective, and business-accommodating administrative climate is basic for intensity. Inordinate administration, defilement, and formality can prevent business development and advancement.

Administration and Political Security: Political dependability and successful administration are fundamental for drawing in speculations and keeping an upper hand. A straightforward and stable political framework diminishes vulnerability and empowers long haul ventures.

Medical services and Prosperity: A sound populace is more useful. Admittance to quality medical services, low infection trouble, and an extravagance and luxury hope are signs of a nation's seriousness.

Ecological Supportability: Intensity shouldn't come to the detriment of the climate. Supportability works on, including environmentally friendly power reception and protection endeavors, assume a part in a country's drawn out seriousness.

Admittance to Fund: An advanced monetary framework that offers admittance to credit and venture capital is pivotal for business development and seriousness.

Comprehensive Approaches: Advancing social incorporation and decreasing pay imbalance is fundamental for long haul seriousness. Comprehensive arrangements guarantee that monetary advantages are extensively shared.

Systems for Upgrading Worldwide Seriousness

Nations trying to upgrade their worldwide seriousness can take on different procedures to address the determinants referenced previously. While every country's methodology might contrast in view of its remarkable conditions and assets, coming up next are a few normal techniques for supporting seriousness:

Put resources into Schooling and Labor force Improvement: States ought to focus on schooling and preparing projects to furnish their residents with the abilities and information expected to contend in a worldwide economy. This remembers speculations for STEM (science, innovation, designing, and math) instruction and professional preparation.

Support Development and Exploration: Empowering innovative work (Research and development) exercises and establishing a steady climate for advancement can prompt mechanical headways, new businesses, and higher intensity. Legislatures can give Research and development awards, charge motivations, and backing for startup environments.

Further develop Framework: Interest in foundation is imperative. This incorporates overhauling transportation organizations, growing broadband access, and modernizing energy frameworks. Upgraded framework diminishes costs, encourages monetary development, and further develops intensity.

Smooth out Guideline: Legislatures ought to attempt to rearrange and smooth out guidelines, lessen administration, and take out defilement. A straightforward and business-accommodating administrative climate draws in ventures and advances seriousness.

Advance Manageable Works on: Empowering natural manageability can improve long haul seriousness. States can carry out approaches that help sustainable power, energy proficiency, and natural preservation.

Encourage Business venture: Supporting a culture of business venture can prompt the making of inventive new companies and private companies. Giving admittance to subsidizing, mentorship, and collaborating spaces can uphold enterprising undertakings.

Put resources into Medical services: Open and top notch medical care is fundamental for a solid and useful labor force. State run administrations ought to put resources into medical care framework and elevate sound ways of life to help intensity.

Upgrade Political Strength and Administration: A stable world of politics and viable administration are appealing to financial backers. Legislatures ought to focus on straightforwardness, law and order, and the insurance of property freedoms.

Receptiveness to Worldwide Exchange: Nations ought to embrace worldwide exchange and diminish exchange boundaries to get to bigger business sectors. Two-sided and multilateral economic alliance can work with worldwide exchange and improve intensity.

Empower Monetary Consideration: Extending admittance to monetary administrations can assist private ventures and people with getting to credit and speculations, advancing financial development and seriousness.

Put resources into Basic Businesses: Distinguishing and supporting enterprises with an upper hand can encourage financial development. Legislatures can give motivating forces to key ventures, like innovation, fabricating, or environmentally friendly power.

Cultivate Social Consideration: Decreasing pay disparity and guaranteeing that the advantages of monetary development are extensively shared is basic for intensity. Social strategies, for example, designated government assistance programs, can assist with accomplishing this objective.

Chapter 8

The Future of Indian Manufacturing

The eventual fate of Indian assembling holds huge commitment and potential for development, driven by a mix of variables that are molding the worldwide monetary scene. India, with its enormous and young populace, vital area, and developing modern biological system, is ready to turn into a key part in the worldwide assembling area. This change is probably going to be affected by a few vital patterns and difficulties, enveloping innovative headways, strategy changes, and worldwide monetary movements.

One of the essential drivers representing things to come of Indian assembling is innovation. The Fourth Modern Transformation, portrayed by the joining of advanced innovations and mechanization, is adjusting the assembling scene around the world. Indian makers are progressively taking on Industry 4.0 ideas, like the Web of Things (IoT), man-made brainpower (simulated intelligence), and 3D printing, to upgrade efficiency, diminish costs, and further develop item quality. These advancements empower producers to smooth out tasks, lessen human mistake, and answer all the more proficiently to showcase requests.

Besides, India's vigorous programming and IT administrations industry have situated the country as a center for programming based assembling arrangements. The union of conventional assembling and state of the art innovation is encouraging development, and Indian makers are utilizing these advanced instruments to remain serious and enter new business sectors. This innovation driven approach will keep on molding the eventual fate of Indian assembling, considering more noteworthy customization, more limited creation cycles, and improved adaptability to adjust to changing business sector elements.

Moreover, the 'Make in India' drive sent off by the Indian government in 2014 has been a critical strategy driver for the assembling area. The goal of this drive is to make India a worldwide assembling center point by empowering homegrown and unfamiliar speculations. It has prompted a few strategy changes pointed toward working on business processes, diminishing regulatory obstacles, and working on the simplicity of carrying on with work. This drive, joined with the execution of the Labor and products Expense (GST), has made a more bound together and business-accommodating duty system, working with highway exchange and advancing assembling development.

Notwithstanding innovation and strategy changes, segment factors assume a urgent part in molding the eventual fate of Indian assembling. India is home to a tremendous and young labor force, which offers a significant benefit regarding work accessibility and cost intensity. Notwithstanding, to completely use this segment profit, there is a requirement for interest in expertise improvement and training to guarantee that the labor force is furnished with the essential abilities for cutting edge fabricating processes.

Moreover, urbanization and the rising working class in India are driving homegrown utilization. As additional individuals move to urban communities and experience an expansion in extra cash, the interest for a great many made items, from buyer merchandise to vehicles, is on the ascent. This developing shopper market presents a critical chance for Indian makers to take special care of homegrown interest and decrease their dependence on trades.

By the by, difficulties and obstructions should be addressed to open the maximum capacity of Indian assembling. Foundation improvement stays a key worry, as productive coordinated operations and transportation frameworks are fundamental for the consistent development of merchandise inside the nation and for sends out. Interest in framework, including streets, ports, and rail lines, is basic to decrease costs and work on the seriousness of Indian assembling.

Natural maintainability is one more major problem for the eventual fate of Indian assembling. As the world turns out to be progressively aware of the ecological effect of modern cycles, Indian makers should embrace greener practices. This includes decreasing discharges, limiting waste, and executing energy-effective innovations. India's obligation to the Paris Understanding and its aggressive environmentally friendly power targets signal a developing spotlight on maintainability, which will probably shape the assembling scene before very long.

Another basic test is the requirement for nonstop advancement and innovative work (Research and development). While India has gained huge headway in different assembling areas, there is a constant requirement for Research and development ventures to foster state of the art innovations, items, and cycles. Joint efforts between the scholarly world, industry, and government can assist with cultivating development and reinforce the exploration environment in the country.

Worldwide exchange elements likewise assume a critical part coming down the line for Indian assembling. Exchange pressures, protectionist approaches, and international vulnerabilities can influence the worldwide store network, influencing Indian makers' capacity to send out their items. Broadening send out objections, diminishing reliance on a solitary market, and upgrading exchange connections are systems that Indian producers ought to consider to relieve these dangers.

Moreover, the serious scene is advancing quickly, with arising economies like Vietnam and Bangladesh gaining ground in assembling. India necessities to stay serious concerning cost, quality, and proficiency to keep up with its situation in the worldwide market. An emphasis on expertise improvement, quality confirmation, and efficiency improvement is crucial for address these difficulties.

The reception of advanced innovations in assembling isn't restricted to huge ventures; it additionally stretches out to little and medium-sized endeavors (SMEs), which structure the foundation of India's assembling area. Taxpayer supported initiatives, for example, the 'Advanced India' drive plan to advance the utilization of innovation in SMEs, making them more cutthroat and coordinated into worldwide stock chains. Admittance to fund and support for innovation reception will be significant for the development of these more modest makers.

One of the areas that holds monstrous possible in store for Indian assembling is the drug business. India has set up a good foundation for itself as the "drug store of the world" by delivering a critical portion of nonexclusive prescriptions universally. With the world's rising interest for reasonable medical services arrangements, the drug area is set to assume an imperative part in India's assembling scene. Interests in Research and development, quality control, and consistence with global norms will be fundamental for the area's practical development.

The car business is one more key supporter of Indian assembling. India is one of the world's biggest car markets, and a few worldwide auto producers have laid out a huge presence in the country. The shift towards electric vehicles (EVs) and the improvement of EV parts present a chance for India to turn into an assembling center for green portability arrangements. Government impetuses and support for the EV biological system can additionally help this area's development.

The aviation and guard industry is one more region with critical potential. With expanding guard modernization and a push for indigenization, Indian makers can assume a urgent part in creating progressed aviation parts and protection hardware. Coordinated efforts with worldwide aviation goliaths can prepare for innovation move and neighborhood creation, adding to confidence in this area.

Besides, the fate of Indian assembling isn't restricted to actual products. The administrations area, including IT and business process re-appropriating (BPO), assumes an integral part.

These administrations are intently attached to assembling, offering help in regions, for example, production network the board, information examination, and client relationship the executives. As assembling processes become more digitized and interconnected, these administrations will proceed to advance and adjust to industry needs.

The Coronavirus pandemic uncovered weaknesses in worldwide stockpile chains, provoking a reassessment of hazard the board techniques. Indian assembling can jump all over this chance by offering strong and differentiated store network arrangements. By lessening reliance on a solitary source and expanding nearby assembling capacities,

India can situate itself as a dependable and appealing option for worldwide organizations looking for strong store network choices.

Notwithstanding the conventional areas, the fate of Indian assembling additionally holds guarantee in arising regions like biotechnology, nanotechnology, and high level materials. These fields offer open doors for advancement, high-esteem producing, and worldwide seriousness. Vital ventures and joint efforts in these areas can drive India into an administrative role in state of the art innovations.

The eventual fate of Indian assembling is inherently connected to the country's capacity to establish an empowering climate for advancement and business venture. India's new companies and private companies are progressively wandering into imaginative item advancement and assembling. The public authority's 'Startup India' drive and different hatcheries and gas pedals are sustaining a culture of development and business venture.

Moreover, manageability and dependable assembling are becoming fundamental to strategic approaches. Moral and harmless to the ecosystem producing cycles can improve an organization's standing and seriousness in the worldwide market. Indian makers ought to focus on supportability and corporate social obligation to line up with global assumptions.

The fate of Indian assembling is likewise intently attached to worldwide economic alliance and coordinated efforts. Participating in worldwide associations, exchange collusions, and international alliances can open new roads for Indian producers to get to worldwide business sectors and grow their products. These associations can assist with conquering exchange hindrances and facil

8.1. Challenges and Opportunities

In the present quickly developing world, people and associations face a horde of difficulties and potential open doors that shape the manner in which we live, work, and cooperate. These difficulties and open doors are entwined, frequently presenting complex problems that request inventive arrangements. In this paper, we will investigate a portion of the vital difficulties and valuable open doors that characterize our contemporary scene, addressing different parts of society, innovation, economy, and the climate.

One of the most squeezing difficulties within recent memory is environmental change. The World's environment is going through huge and possibly irreversible changes because of the emanation of ozone harming substances. This worldwide issue presents both a grave test and a significant open door. On one hand, the results of inaction are desperate, with rising ocean levels, outrageous climate occasions, and asset shortage undermining the planet's tenability. Then again, tending to environmental change presents a chance for supportable turn of events, green advancement, and worldwide participation. The desperation of the environment emergency forces us to reconsider our energy frameworks, transportation strategies, and utilization designs, catalyzing the improvement of clean energy advances and the reception of more eco-accommodating ways of life.

Another significant test we face is the quick progression of innovation. While mechanical advancement has prompted wonderful developments in correspondence, medical services, and numerous different fields, it additionally delivers difficulties connected with protection, security, and the fate of work. The advanced unrest has reshaped our social orders, offering uncommon network and admittance to data yet in addition raising worries about information breaks, cyberattacks, and the disintegration of protection. Besides, mechanization and computerized reasoning can possibly uproot a huge number of occupations, requiring a reexamination of our labor force and the improvement of new abilities. Simultaneously, these mechanical difficulties present open doors for people and associations to bridle the force of advancement, make new organizations, and change the manner in which we work and live.

The worldwide economy is another domain full of difficulties and amazing open doors. Pay imbalance, exchange strains, and monetary unsteadiness are among the difficulties that plague the financial scene. The inconsistent dispersion of abundance and assets presents moral and social quandaries, as it can prompt social distress and political unsteadiness. In the mean time, exchange debates between countries can upset worldwide stock chains and obstruct financial development. In any case, these financial difficulties are not unconquerable, and they present open doors for creative monetary arrangements and social changes. Legislatures and associations get the opportunity to address pay disparity, advance fair exchange rehearses, and make more impartial monetary frameworks that benefit all citizenry.

In the domain of medical services, the world is wrestling with the difficulties and potential open doors presented by a quickly maturing populace and the continuous Coronavirus pandemic. Maturing populaces deliver issues connected with medical services costs, providing care, and benefits frameworks. The rising interest for medical care administrations can strain assets and framework, making it fundamental to advance in medical care conveyance and foster more productive and savvy therapies. Then again, the Coronavirus pandemic, while a stupendous test, has sped up the turn of events and reception of telemedicine, remote work, and immunization innovation. These advances in medical care conveyance, innovation, and logical exploration can possibly change medical care frameworks and work on worldwide wellbeing in the long haul.

Instruction, as well, faces a large group of difficulties and open doors. Admittance to quality training isn't equally conveyed, making differences in information and potential open doors. This imbalance can block social versatility and breaking point the capability of people who need admittance to instructive assets. Notwithstanding, progressions in web based learning, open instructive assets, and advanced devices can possibly democratize training, making it more available and reasonable to individuals around the world. These mechanical advancements offer open doors for long lasting learning, abilities improvement, and the worldwide trade of information.

Moreover, the difficulties and open doors in the field of computerized reasoning and AI are critical. Computer based intelligence can possibly upgrade our lives through applications in medical services, money, transportation, and numerous different areas. In any case, it likewise raises worries about morals, predisposition, and occupation removal. The mindful turn of events and organization of computer based intelligence innovations are fundamental for bridle the amazing open doors while relieving the dangers. Challenges connected with morals and predisposition in simulated intelligence frameworks feature the requirement for different points of view, moral rules, and guidelines to guarantee that simulated intelligence benefits society overall.

Social and political difficulties are likewise fundamental to our contemporary scene. Issues connected with civil rights, racial imbalance, and political polarization have arrived at basic points. These difficulties are in many cases well established in verifiable shameful acts and can prompt social agitation and political precariousness. Regardless, they present open doors for foundational change, exchange, and the progression of additional comprehensive and fair social orders. Grassroots developments, strategy changes, and global participation can possibly address these difficulties and make an additional fair and amicable world.

In the domain of international affairs, the difficulties and open doors are similarly perplexing. International pressures, clashes, and security concerns persevere all over the planet, raising the phantom of worldwide shakiness. Simultaneously, worldwide collaboration, strategy, and compromise endeavors offer open doors for harmony, security, and worldwide advancement. Issues like atomic demilitarization, environment arrangements, and compassionate intercessions highlight the significance of cooperating to address shared worldwide difficulties.

One more diverse test is the relocation and removal of individuals, driven by elements, for example, struggle, environmental change, and monetary inconsistencies. The predicament of outcasts and travelers is a philanthropic emergency that tests our aggregate limit with regards to compassion and fortitude. While movement presents difficulties connected with line security, social combination, and asset assignment, it additionally offers amazing open doors to feature our mankind by giving wellbeing, assurance, and valuable open doors for those out of luck.

The universe of business and business venture faces its own arrangement of difficulties and open doors. Market rivalry, monetary vulnerability, and changing purchaser inclinations can introduce impressive difficulties to organizations. In any case, these difficulties additionally encourage advancement, rivalry, and the improvement of items and administrations that address developing issues. New businesses and laid out organizations the same get the opportunity to adjust, turn, and flourish in this powerful scene.

Manageability and natural protection are fundamental difficulties and chances within recent memory. The exhaustion of regular assets, contamination, and territory obliteration compromise the fragile equilibrium of our planet's biological systems. Environmental change, species elimination, and deforestation are basic worries that require prompt consideration. Notwithstanding, they additionally present open doors for manageable practices, sustainable power sources, and protection endeavors that can save the planet for people in the future. The push for supportable turn of events and eco-accommodating innovations isn't just a moral objective yet in addition a promising road for financial development and occupation creation.

In the field of worldwide relations, the difficulties and open doors related with globalization are ever-present. While globalization has prompted expanded interconnectedness and the free progression of thoughts, products, and data, it has likewise raised worries about social homogenization, monetary reliance, and the disintegration of neighborhood enterprises. By and by, globalization offers potential open doors for multifaceted trade, monetary participation, and the sharing of information that can cultivate common comprehension and financial turn of events.

The difficulties and open doors in the field of room investigation are really unlimited. As humankind adventures past Earth, we experience difficulties connected with the tremendous distances, outrageous circumstances, and the distribution of assets for space attempts. Nonetheless, the investigation of room opens up the chance of logical disclosures, asset use, and the potential for future residence of other divine bodies. Space innovations and examination offer a door to logical progression and global cooperation that can reshape how we might interpret the universe.

Training and the spread of data face their own arrangement of difficulties and valuable open doors in the advanced age. Deception and the spread of phony news present critical difficulties to informed direction and cultural union. In any case, computerized stages, virtual entertainment, and online networks give open doors for the trading of suggestions, worldwide cooperation, and metro commitment. Advancing media proficiency and capable internet based conduct while utilizing the capability of these stages for positive change is fundamental.

The difficulties and valuable open doors related with medical care are especially articulated with regards to worldwide wellbeing emergencies. Irresistible sicknesses, as exemplified by the Coronavirus pandemic, challenge medical services frameworks and worldwide participation.

Nonetheless, they likewise highlight the requirement for worldwide wellbeing security, logical coordinated effort, and the improvement of quick reaction systems to address future pandemics. Propels in antibody improvement, clinical exploration, and medical care conveyance can possibly.

8.2. Emerging Trends and Technologies

Arising patterns and advancements are constantly reshaping the manner in which we live, work, and communicate in our quickly developing world. These advancements length different areas, including science, designing, medical services, correspondence, and that's just the beginning. In this exposition, we will investigate the absolute most unmistakable arising patterns and advancements that are molding the present and future, addressing their effect on society, the economy, and people.

Computerized reasoning (simulated intelligence) is at the bleeding edge of the mechanical unrest. It incorporates AI, normal language handling, and PC vision, permitting machines to perform undertakings that commonly require human knowledge. Artificial intelligence is progressively incorporated into different areas, from medical services to back, mechanizing processes, making expectations, and improving navigation. The development of computer based intelligence has been joined by worries about morals, predisposition, and security. Moral contemplations are vital as computer based intelligence frameworks progressively impact our lives, from work enlistment calculations to independent vehicles. Finding some kind of harmony between mechanical progression and moral principles is one of the best difficulties within recent memory.

AI, a subset of man-made intelligence, is a quickly developing field that empowers PCs to gain and improve for a fact without being unequivocally customized. AI models, including profound learning brain organizations, have been applied to different applications like picture acknowledgment, language interpretation, and suggestion frameworks. These innovations groundbreakingly affect ventures like web based business, medical services, and diversion. The proceeded with improvement of AI calculations and the accessibility of enormous datasets are driving the field forward, promising significantly more refined applications later on.

The Web of Things (IoT) addresses the organization of interconnected gadgets, vehicles, structures, and different items that can gather and trade information. This interconnectedness is reforming businesses, from savvy homes and urban communities to agribusiness and assembling. IoT gadgets are utilized for checking, control, and robotization, prompting further developed proficiency and accommodation. Nonetheless, the expansion of IoT gadgets likewise raises worries about information protection and security, as every gadget presents a potential section point for cyberattacks. Finding some kind of harmony between the advantages of IoT and the requirement for security is a continuous test.

Blockchain innovation, at first produced for digital currencies like Bitcoin, is getting momentum in different businesses past money. Blockchain is a decentralized and disseminated record framework that gives straightforwardness, security, and confidence in exchanges. Its applications reach out to production network the executives, casting a ballot frameworks, and medical services records, where information uprightness and credibility are critical. As blockchain develops, it can possibly upset how information and resources are confirmed and moved, decreasing the requirement for delegates. Nonetheless, the innovation isn't without its difficulties, including adaptability and administrative worries.

5G innovation is the up and coming age of remote correspondence, promising quicker speeds, lower inertness, and more prominent network. This innovation can possibly empower different applications, from increased reality (AR) and augmented reality (VR) to independent vehicles and distant medical procedure. Notwithstanding, the rollout of 5G organizations presents difficulties connected with framework, security, and range designation. The expanded network and information transmission capacities of 5G will without a doubt influence how we convey, work, and engage ourselves.

Quantum registering is an arising field that use the standards of quantum mechanics to deal with data in manners unimaginable for old style PCs. Quantum PCs can possibly tackle complex issues in cryptography, drug revelation, and advancement that are as of now past the compass of customary registering. The improvement of quantum PCs is still in its beginning phases, with various specialized difficulties to survive, for example, keeping up with quantum rationality and blunder remedy. Once developed, quantum registering could alter enterprises and fields as different as materials science and computerized reasoning.

Biotechnology, including quality altering and manufactured science, is at the front line of logical development. CRISPR-Cas9, a progressive quality altering device, can possibly fix hereditary sicknesses, change life forms, and improve crop yields. The force of biotechnology brings up issues about morals, guideline, and the potential for unseen side-effects. As we explore the moral and administrative scene, biotechnology presents chances to address wellbeing and natural difficulties in remarkable ways.

Environmentally friendly power sources, for example, sunlight based and wind power, are changing the energy scene. The progress to sustainable power is fundamental for relieving environmental change and lessening reliance on petroleum derivatives. The moderateness and effectiveness of sustainable innovations have improved, making them progressively cutthroat with conventional energy sources. Be that as it may, challenges stay in energy capacity, matrix joining, and strategy support. The worldwide shift toward sustainable power isn't just a natural goal yet additionally a financial chance for advancement and occupation creation.

Expanded Reality (AR) and Augmented Reality (VR) are vivid advancements that modify our impression of the actual world. AR overlays advanced data onto this present reality, while VR establishes altogether virtual conditions.

The two advances have applications in gaming, schooling, preparing, and medical care. AR improves our everyday encounters, from route applications to intuitive promoting. VR, then again, transports clients to virtual domains, giving better approaches to learn, investigate, and mingle. These advances can possibly reshape how we collaborate with data and our general surroundings.

Mechanical Interaction Computerization (RPA) is an innovation that robotizes dull errands by utilizing programming robots. It is especially significant in businesses like money, medical care, and client assistance, where manual cycles can be tedious and mistake inclined. RPA upgrades efficiency, diminishes human blunder, and liberates workers to zero in on additional imaginative and vital errands. The innovation's true capacity is tremendous, however it likewise presents difficulties connected with work relocation and the requirement for upskilling the labor force.

Biometrics and facial acknowledgment innovations have progressed quickly and are presently incorporated into regular day to day existence, from opening cell phones to confirming personality at air terminals. These advances offer expanded security and accommodation, yet they additionally raise worries about protection and observation. Finding some kind of harmony between the advantages of biometrics and the requirement for individual privileges and information security is a squeezing cultural issue.

Regenerative medication, including foundational microorganism treatment and tissue designing, holds the commitment of fixing and recovering harmed or deteriorated tissues and organs. This field can possibly change medical services by giving new therapies to conditions like coronary illness, spinal line wounds, and diabetes. Notwithstanding, moral contemplations, administrative difficulties, and the requirement for thorough clinical preliminaries are basic to the dependable improvement of regenerative medication.

Independent vehicles, including self-driving vehicles and robots, are reforming transportation. These advancements can possibly decrease auto collisions, increment transportation proficiency, and further develop availability for people with restricted versatility. Be that as it may, the broad reception of independent vehicles requires tending to somewhere safe, administrative, and moral worries. The shift to independent transportation addresses a tremendous change by they way we move individuals and products.

Space investigation keeps on catching our creative mind and rouse logical disclosure. With the developing interest in Mars investigation, the potential for mining space rocks, and the appearance of business space travel, mankind is nearly extraordinary accomplishments in space. Notwithstanding, space investigation is loaded with difficulties, including the significant expense, the potential for space trash, and the requirement for global participation. The quest for space investigation presents valuable open doors for logical progression, financial development, and the possibility to guarantee the endurance of the human species past Earth.

Neurotechnology, like cerebrum PC interfaces and neuroimaging, is opening new boondocks in understanding and cooperating with the human mind. These advances have applications in medical services, gaming, and correspondence. Mind PC interfaces, specifically, offer the possibility to reestablish versatility and correspondence for people with inabilities. As neurotechnology propels, it suggests conversation starters about protection, security, and the potential for mental improvement.

8.3. Potential for Growth and Leadership

The potential for development and initiative is an essential part of any individual, association, or country's excursion towards success and progress. This exposition dives into the open doors and difficulties that underlie the journey for development and authority in the present dynamic and interconnected world, tending to different aspects like monetary development, advancement, administration, and global relations.

Financial development is a central component of progress. It envelops the extension of an economy's result, work creation, and the improvement of expectations for everyday comforts. Financial development is driven by factors like venture, mechanical progression, and exchange. In any case, accomplishing supportable financial development isn't without its difficulties. Monetary cycles, like downturns and monetary emergencies, can upset development directions. Pay imbalance, asset shortage, and natural debasement represent extra difficulties that should be addressed to guarantee that development helps all fragments of society and doesn't come to the detriment of people in the future.

Development is a critical driver of development and thriving. Development involves the making of groundbreaking thoughts, items, and cycles that can prompt expanded efficiency and seriousness. Advancements can go from mechanical forward leaps to new plans of action, and they frequently rise up out of joint effort, exploration, and chance taking. Empowering development requires encouraging a steady environment that incorporates instruction, examination, business, and admittance to capital. While development can push economies and associations forward, it likewise presents difficulties connected with protected innovation, morals, and the requirement for persistent variation in a quickly impacting world.

Administration is indispensable to guiding people, associations, and countries toward their development potential. Compelling pioneers move and guide others, settling on essential choices, defining objectives, and making a common vision. Administration isn't exclusively the area of those in proper, influential places; it tends to be shown by people at all levels. Be that as it may, administration isn't without its difficulties. Pioneers should wrestle with issues like moral problems, the requirement for responsibility, and the interest for versatility despite affliction. Creating pioneers who can explore these difficulties while cultivating development and advancement is a basic undertaking for social orders and associations.

Globalization has changed the scene of worldwide relations, offering the two open doors and difficulties for countries and associations the same. The interconnectedness of the worldwide economy, data stream, and global governmental issues can possibly work with collaboration, exchange, and innovative trade. Simultaneously, globalization has prompted expanded contest, international pressures, and the potential for monetary interdependencies to make weaknesses. Countries and associations should explore the intricacies of worldwide interconnection and encourage global relations that advance development and soundness.

Mechanical headway is a focal main impetus behind development and initiative in the cutting edge world. Innovation can upgrade efficiency, empower new ventures, and reshape the manner in which individuals live and work. The Fourth Modern

Upheaval, portrayed by the coordination of computerized innovations, man-made reasoning, and the Web of Things, is changing ventures going from medical services to assembling. Tackling the capability of innovation is crucial for development and initiative, however it accompanies difficulties connected with network protection, information security, and the need to guarantee that mechanical progressions benefit society in general.

Training assumes a major part in supporting development and initiative potential. An accomplished people is furnished with the abilities and information expected to drive development, add to monetary development, and take on influential positions. Nonetheless, differences in instructive access and quality present huge difficulties to numerous people and networks. Spanning these instructive holes, advancing deep rooted learning, and adjusting to the changing requests of the gig market are fundamental parts of cultivating development and authority in the present quickly developing world.

Ecological supportability is a basic that should be viewed as in any conversation of development and administration. The consumption of regular assets, living space obliteration, and environmental change are difficulties that compromise the planet's drawn out soundness. Seeking after development and authority should line up with standards of maintainability, incorporating environmentally friendly power sources, mindful asset the board, and preservation endeavors. The change to a reasonable future isn't simply a moral decision; likewise a monetary open door can drive development, make green positions, and upgrade the personal satisfaction for current and people in the future.

In the domain of business and business venture, development and authority are firmly entwined. Organizations, whether new companies or laid out partnerships, try to grow their activities, increment portion of the overall industry, and convey creative items and administrations. Initiative inside associations is fundamental for setting vital course, cultivating a culture of development, and propelling representatives to accomplish their maximum capacity. Notwithstanding, organizations likewise face difficulties as market rivalry, changing purchaser inclinations, and monetary vulnerability. Compelling initiative that can adjust to these difficulties while driving development is a sign of fruitful associations.

The development of environmentally friendly power sources, for example, sun oriented and wind power, is a perfect representation of how innovation, manageability, and monetary development meet. The progress to environmentally friendly power is fundamental for alleviating environmental change and diminishing reliance on non-renewable energy sources. The reasonableness and productivity of inexhaustible innovations have improved, making them progressively serious with conventional energy sources. Thus, the shift to sustainable power addresses a natural basic as well as a monetary chance for development and occupation creation.

Man-made consciousness (computer based intelligence) is one more innovation that holds huge potential for development and authority. Artificial intelligence incorporates AI, normal language handling, and PC vision, permitting machines to perform assignments that ordinarily require human knowledge. The development of artificial intelligence has been joined by worries about morals, predisposition, and protection. Moral contemplations are foremost as artificial intelligence frameworks progressively impact our lives, from work enrollment calculations to independent vehicles. Finding some kind of harmony between innovative headway and moral principles is one of the best difficulties within recent memory.

Development is the backbone of development and administration, and it is intently attached to innovation. Advancement includes the formation of groundbreaking thoughts, items, and cycles that can prompt expanded efficiency and intensity. Developments can go from innovative forward leaps to new plans of action, and they frequently rise out of joint effort, examination, and hazard taking. Empowering development requires encouraging a strong environment that incorporates training, examination, business venture, and admittance to capital. While development can impel economies and associations forward, it likewise presents difficulties connected with licensed innovation, morals, and the requirement for consistent transformation in a quickly impacting world.

The Web of Things (IoT) addresses an innovation that can possibly drive development and initiative across different areas. IoT involves the organization of interconnected gadgets, vehicles, structures, and different articles that can gather and trade information. This interconnectedness is reforming enterprises, from brilliant homes and urban communities to farming and assembling. IoT gadgets are utilized for observing, control, and robotization, prompting further developed effectiveness and comfort. Nonetheless, the expansion of IoT gadgets likewise raises worries about information protection and security, as every gadget presents a potential passage point for cyberattacks. Finding some kind of harmony between the advantages of IoT and the requirement for security is a continuous test.

Blockchain innovation, at first created for digital currencies like Bitcoin, is getting some decent momentum in different businesses past money. Blockchain is a decentralized and dispersed record framework that gives straightforwardness, security, and confidence in exchanges. Its applications reach out to store network the executives, casting a ballot frameworks, and medical services records, where information honesty and credibility are significant.

As blockchain develops, it can possibly upset how information and resources are confirmed and moved, diminishing the requirement for go-betweens. Be that as it may, the innovation isn't without its difficulties, including versatility and administrative worries.

Authority is crucial for exploring the intricacies of development, advancement, and change. Successful pioneers move and guide others, pursuing vital choices, defining objectives, and making a common vision. Administration isn't exclusively the space of those in proper, influential places; it tends to be shown by people at all levels. Nonetheless, initiative isn't without its difficulties.

www.ingramcontent.com/pod-product-compliance
Lightning Source LLC
Chambersburg PA
CBHW071352230926
51846CB00002B/524
* 9 7 8 8 1 9 6 7 2 3 6 7 5 *